Heatstroke

A comedy

Eric Chappell

Samuel French — London
New York - Toronto - Hollywood

HEATSTROKE

First produced in translation by the Riksteatern Company of Sweden in February 1999, *Heatstroke* enjoyed a highly successful nine month tour of the country, taking in Stockholm and Gothenburg. The original cast was:

Sam Spencer	Lakke Magnusson
Fay Spencer	Christine Stenius
Howard Booth	Ulf Brunnberg
Dodie	Åsa Danielson
Raynor	Per-Gunnar Hylén
Moon	Kåre Mölder

Directed by Björn Gustafson

CHARACTERS

Sam Spencer; about 50
Fay Spencer; younger than Sam
Howard Booth, an actor; about 50
Dodie, an actress, Howard's girlfriend; mid-20s
Raynor, powerfully built; 30s
Moon; small, dapper; 30s
Englishwoman (unscripted voice only)
Two **Spanish Policemen** (non-speaking)

The action of the play takes place in the living-room and on the adjoining terrace of a villa in south-east Spain

Time: the present

SYNOPSIS OF SCENES

ACT I   Late afternoon

ACT II
    Scene 1   A few minutes later
    Scene 2   Late evening

Also by Eric Chappell,
published by Samuel French Ltd

Haunted
Haywire
It Can Damage Your Health
Natural Causes
Theft

ACT I

A villa in south-east Spain. High summer. Late afternoon

In the foreground is a spacious living-room with a door L, leading off to the hall, kitchen and bedrooms, and sliding patio doors giving on to a terrace. The living-room has a tiled floor, bamboo and wicker furniture, a drinks cabinet, and a television set DR; all the furniture is angled towards the television

The terrace is edged by a low stone wall topped with iron railings and covered with bougainvillaea. Steps from the centre of the terrace lead down L and R to an unseen swimming pool. Ornamental lights adorn the stone pillars either side of the steps. There are a table and chairs on the terrace together with holiday paraphernalia for beach and garden: a beach bag (containing snorkels, flippers and a bathing hat), balls, croquet mallets, a sombrero on a stand and other items. There is also a garden brush

In the distance is the rolling landscape of the Sierra Blanca

When the CURTAIN rises, the sliding patio doors are open to the terrace and bags and cases, including an airport carrier bag and a distinctive blue holdall, are littered about the room. Fay's handbag is on a table

Sam Spencer enters abruptly up the steps from the pool. He is a harassed figure, aged about fifty, in a crumpled suit. He looks shaken

Sam Fay! (*He crosses to the airport bag and begins opening a bottle*)

Fay Spencer enters. She has already slipped into shorts and top. Her blonde hair is set in a short holiday perm. She is younger than her husband, more thoughtful, and clearly the organizer

Fay I thought you were going to change? Isn't it wonderful? I knew it would be when I saw the photographs. It's the Garden of Eden, Sam.
Sam (*grimly*) Is it?
Fay What's the matter?
Sam If it's the Garden of Eden, I've just seen the serpent.

Fay What?
Sam A snake — down by the swimming pool.
Fay A snake. How big?
Sam About the size of an average garden hose.
Fay Are you sure?
Sam I didn't stay to measure it.

Fay considers this for a moment

Fay Perhaps it was a garden hose?
Sam It wasn't just lying there, Fay. It was upright and doing a rumba. It was either dancing with another snake or tying itself in bloody knots.
Fay It's probably a mating ritual.
Sam Don't tell me the buggers are going to breed.
Fay (*peering over the railings*) You probably won't see it again; the villa was empty last week. They must have moved in when it was quiet; they'll soon move off.
Sam Don't you believe it. They've probably taken the place for the summer. Invited a few friends in, mixed some dry martinis — just started the dancing when we arrived. I didn't like the way he looked at me, Fay.
Fay He was probably more frightened of you than you were of him.
Sam Then he must have been petrified.
Fay Where did he go?
Sam He crawled into the bougainvillaea at the foot of the steps.
Fay There you are, he was more frightened; you weren't the one who crawled into the bougainvillaea, were you? Now calm down and help me unpack.

Sam takes the bottles from the airport bag

Fay No, not the bottles, Sam. I know you'll help me with those. I meant the cases.
Sam (*darkly*) The foot of the left-hand steps — just remember that.
Fay We'll avoid them. Now relax.
Sam I just don't see why we had to come during the snake season.
Fay We didn't have any choice. It was a cancellation — and it's not as if it's costing us anything. First bedroom on the right …

Sam picks up some cases and exits. He returns almost at once without the cases

Sam Yes, I've been thinking about that. There must be a snag, Fay.
Fay (*cautiously*) Why?
Sam Well, you've worked for Sidney for ten years; he's never offered you the villa before.

Fay Well, it's usually reserved for clients, but the client cancelled.

Sam But why you? Why were you selected?

Fay Well, he knows we've had a bad year ——

Sam Bad year. (*Suspiciously*) What have you told him?

Fay I didn't tell him anything, but he sort of heard — about your demotion.

Sam Demotion! It wasn't a demotion. It was a sideways move.

Fay But for less money.

Sam (*after a pause*) As it so happens — yes. But there are fringe benefits and I'm allowed to maintain my superannuation payments at the same level.

Fay But out of less money.

Sam I wish you hadn't told him. He'll think I'm a failure.

Fay No, he won't. He knows you've been under a great deal of strain — losing both your parents in the same year. And then there's the dog. I mean what's going to happen when his back legs finally go, Sam?

Sam I don't know. I suppose we'll have to push him round in a trolley. God! I seem to be surrounded by ageing these days.

Fay I hope I'm not included in that remark.

Sam No, but it's made me realize how short life is, Fay.

Fay Well, your parents were in their nineties.

Sam That doesn't make it any easier. They were always there — now I'm an orphan. It's made me think. I need to review my life. Find myself.

Fay That's why we're here. The trouble is you can't relax … (*She looks through her handbag. NB: For the rest of the play she keeps the bag with her at all times*)

Sam If you want me to relax stop looking through your handbag. I keep thinking you've lost something.

Fay (*after a pause*) Oh …

Sam (*panicking*) What! Is it the passports?

Fay No … It's all right. I've found them.

Sam God! I wish you'd stop doing that.

Fay You just don't like holidays, Sam — you'd much sooner be creosoting the fence.

Sam I've nothing against holidays, Fay. I enjoy holidays. It's holidaymakers I can't stand. Like that smug bastard at the airport. The one in the linen jacket with the cuffs rolled back, the Gucci sneakers, the straw hat and the medallion and the sunglasses — and that was in the pouring rain at Gatwick!

Fay I didn't see him.

Sam You were too busy looking through your handbag. (*Grimly*) But I was watching him. Do you know something? He was the only person on that plane to tip his seat back. The poor devil behind him got his lunch tray straight in his lap.

Fay (*smiling*) You *were* watching him, weren't you?

Sam And he was first off the plane. He had a trolley as soon as he touched terra firma. How did he do that?

Fay Perhaps it was collapsible.

Sam And he was first through passport control. I didn't catch up with him until we got to the carousel. That's when we had the confrontation.

Fay I didn't know you had a confrontation.

Sam You were in the "Señoras". He tried to take my holdall — the blue one. I said, "Excuse me, Buster, that holdall happens to be mine." He went down like a pricked balloon.

Fay (*smiling*) That must have been very satisfying.

Sam It was. And we beat him through Customs. And we got our hired car before him. Which shows the race isn't always to the swiftest, Fay. (*He smiles*) I saw him standing outside the airport as we drove away. I waved. He looked shit-stricken.

Fay Well, that should have put you in a good mood.

Sam It's given me an appetite. Anything to eat?

Fay The villa people have left a starter pack in the kitchen …

Sam exits

Sam (*off*) There's not much …

Fay We'll have to go down to the *supermercado* for the rest.

Sam enters eating cheese

Sam Super what?

Fay Mercado. Supermarket.

Sam (*frowning*) I hope you're not going to start speaking Spanish, Fay.

Fay Why not?

Sam Because I won't understand you.

Fay Sam, we have to know a few phrases. We're not package — this isn't Benidorm. This is the Spanish countryside. I asked you to read the phrase book.

Sam I can make myself understood. I have very eloquent hand movements.

Fay (*drily*) Yes — I noticed one or two when we drove from the airport. But that's not the point. The point is will you understand them. (*She takes the phrase book from her handbag*) Suppose you're in the sea and someone shouts … (*Reading; dramatically*) *"Cuidade – vienne coma ole grande!"* What would you do?

Sam I don't know.

Fay Precisely. And by the time you did know — it would be too late.

Sam Why?

Fay Because it means, "Look out — there's a big wave coming", and you'd be swept out to sea. Read the book.

Fay throws the book to Sam

Fay takes another case through to the bedroom

Sam sits and reads the phrase book

Sam Lord! Fay, listen. "Useful phrases."

Fay returns

Secorro! Help! *Hay fuego*! Fire! *Ladron*. Thief. *Detengale*! Stop him! *Dejeme*. Leave me alone. *Basta*! That will do. *Marchese*. Go away. What sort of holiday are we expecting here?

Fay Just learn to ask for the lavatory because you won't hear much English spoken here.

Sam The woman in the bottom villa's English.

Fay (*surprised*) How do you know?

Sam She spoke to me.

Fay (*concerned*) But I understood they were Spanish. She must be new.

Sam (*grinning*) She was sunbathing — in the nude.

Fay You mean in full view?

Sam No — you have to stand on that low wall ...

Fay (*coolly*) Was this before you saw the snake or after?

Sam Before. Why?

Fay Only you mentioned the serpent — you didn't say you'd seen Eve.

Sam At least she's English. Perhaps we'll see more of her.

Fay I don't see how you could, Sam.

Sam I meant she could show us the ropes.

Fay If she suggests anything with ropes, Sam — make yourself scarce.

Sam The funny thing was she thought she knew me. She called me Howard.

Fay (*with a start*) Howard?

Sam Yes.

Fay (*anxiously*) What did you say?

Sam (*puzzled*) I didn't say anything.

Fay Good.

Sam (*suspiciously*) What do you mean — good?

Fay Nothing.

Sam You're hiding something.

Fay No. (*She looks into her handbag*)

Sam Then why are you looking in your handbag? You always do that when you're hiding something. What did you mean when you said "Good"?

Fay (*after a hesitation*) It's because ...

Sam Yes?

Fay (*slowly*) Because — we're not really supposed to be here ...

Silence

Sam Not what?

Fay Supposed to be here.

Sam Would you say that again, Fay. I don't understand. Perhaps if you said it in Spanish.

Fay You know what I mean.

Sam No, I don't know what you mean. Not supposed to be here. Where am I supposed to be?

Fay Creosoting the fence.

Sam You mean Sidney doesn't know we're here?

Fay No … Not exactly. He knows someone's supposed to be here — but not us.

Sam Fay, who is supposed to be here?

Fay Howard Booth.

Sam Howard … !

Fay Booth. But he cancelled. His wife rang to say he couldn't make it. Sidney was in LA and I couldn't contact him — and there was a spare set of keys in the office — and …

Sam Yes?

Fay And I knew you were having a few days off to creosote the fence. And I thought — what the hell.

Sam What the hell! What the hell! I'll tell you what the hell. We're trespassing, Fay. So that's why she called me Howard. She was expecting Howard Booth.

Fay I suppose so.

Sam Do I look like Howard Booth?

Fay No. He's taller for one thing.

Sam She didn't seem to notice.

Fay Well, you were standing on a wall, Sam.

Sam I can't spend the whole week standing on a wall, Fay.

Fay Just don't get intimate with her.

Sam Fay, she walks around naked. We're bound to get intimate. Then there's the villa people: the maid, the pool man, the gardener. Are they all expecting Howard Booth?

Fay I don't know, but it's not as if you're going to get close to people.

Sam Isn't it?

Fay No.

Sam considers this

Sam Well, I suppose if anyone called I could always submerge myself in the pool and breathe through a straw.

Fay There's no need for that. No-one knows what Howard Booth looks like now, not these days.

Sam But he's an actor, isn't he?

Fay Sam, let me ask you something. Do you know what he looks like?

Sam No, but I don't watch television.

Fay He hasn't been on television in years. Not since the seventies. He played Seth Warren, the gamekeeper in "Green Acres" — until he shot himself in a covert. He didn't do much after that. In fact, he went off the rails.

Sam Why?

Fay Woman trouble. He's been married three times.

Sam Three times! (*Bitterly*) My God! Isn't once enough?

Fay (*reproachfully*) Sam.

Sam Sorry, but it has been a bit of a shock, Fay.

Fay Well, at least one good thing's come out of it — you've stopped worrying about the snake.

Sam Fay, if Sidney finds out you could lose your job.

Fay I suppose so.

Sam (*his voice getting louder and louder during the following*) Suppose so! We have a hundred and fifty pounds in the bank and our whole existence is based on two pay packets — and you suppose so?

Fay (*quietly*) Sam, sit down; let me talk to you.

Fay sits Sam down

You've been tense and irritable for weeks — and it's been getting worse. That's why I brought you here. I don't know what's going on in your mind because you won't tell me but when we get back I'm going to get your blood pressure checked. Until then, try and relax.

Sam Relax! First the snake — and then this. What else? These things always go in threes, Fay.

Fay Sam, let's live dangerously for once.

Sam Fay, how can I live dangerously and relax at the same time?

Fay looks through her handbag

Fay — you're looking in your handbag again?

Fay I was looking for the key to your blue holdall.

Sam I've got it. Why?

Sam hands Fay the key

Fay Before we set off you said you had a surprise for me. I want to see it.

Sam (*uneasily*) I just hope you don't think I've been rash ...

Fay Of course I won't.

Sam It was an impulse ...

Fay Now I'm intrigued … (*She tries to open the blue holdall, but struggles with the lock*) Funny — it's jammed …

Sam Let me do it.

Fay No — I can wiggle it …

Sam Fay, you're forcing it — you're ruining a perfectly good holdall… (*She opens the holdall with a snap. She looks in and then stares at Sam*) What's the matter?

Fay I think I've found the third thing. You fool, Sam.

Sam What?

Fay There must be a fortune here in twenty-pound notes.

Sam (*moving to Fay*) What are you talking about?

Fay You've sold the house, haven't you? You always said you would and now you've done it.

Sam (*staring into the holdall*) My God!

Fay We're homeless, aren't we, Sam?

Sam Don't be silly, Fay. I haven't sold the house. I couldn't — it's in joint title. I couldn't sell it without your agreement.

Fay How do you know? Have you tried?

Sam No; besides, it wouldn't have fetched all this. There must be a fortune here in twenty-pound notes.

Fay I've just said that.

Sam Fay, I don't know anything about it.

Fay Then why were you so secretive? What did you put in the holdall?

Sam Well, I spent more than I meant to. There was a couple of silk shirts, a cashmere sweater, and a cologne — Givenchy for Men …

Fay Givenchy for Men?

Sam Yes.

Fay I thought you'd come here to find yourself?

Sam I have.

Fay Well, you won't have much trouble finding yourself — not with Givenchy for Men.

Sam I knew you wouldn't approve; that's why ——

Fay Wait a minute! This isn't your holdall. Look, there's a piece of red string around the handle — probably where the label was attached …

Sam You're right. Then whose is it?

Fay I think I know. Remember the smug bastard at the airport? Who thought this was his holdall? Remember, "Excuse me, Buster — that holdall happens to be mine"? Well, it wasn't — it was his. No wonder he looked shit-stricken.

Sam What are we going to do?

Fay I'll tell you what we're going to do. We're going to drive into Javea and hand this over to the police.

Sam restrains Fay

Sam Wait a minute, Fay. Let's think about this.

Fay What's there to think about?

Sam There's a fortune here in twenty-pound notes.

Fay Don't keep saying that!

Sam There could be half a million.

Fay Half a million!

Sam There could be a problem.

Fay What problem?

Sam (*slowly*) This is English money and we're in Spain …

Fay Well, once we've handed it over it's their problem.

Sam Don't you believe it. We could spend the rest of the holiday at the police station — being interrogated. And we're not even supposed to be here. I should be cresosoting the fence. There'll be publicity. "Honest — if stupid — holiday-makers return a fortune in —— "

Fay Don't say that again! All right, we'll have to drive back to the airport and find the smug bastard, won't we?

Sam All the way to Alicante? Besides, how did he come by the money, Fay? Have you thought about that?

Fay I don't know.

Sam Not honestly. I think he was in illegal possession of this money.

Fay You mean like we are?

Sam No, not like we are. If he's a criminal, Fay, he won't be hanging around there to be picked up.

Fay Then we'll hand it over to the airport authorities.

Sam We'll still have to answer a lot of questions, at the end of which we'll still be out of pocket.

Fay Out of pocket?

Sam He's got my shirts, Fay.

Fay That's right! He's probably got your holdall. He'll trace you. He's probably on his way here now. My God!

Sam Calm down. Fay. (*Slowly*) There's nothing in that holdall he could trace back to me …

Fay (*studying Sam*) You're going to keep it, aren't you?

Sam No. I'm simply waiting for it to be claimed.

Fay How can he claim it? He doesn't know who's got it.

Sam I'm not denying I've got it but I'm not going to shout it from the rooftops — that could lead to spurious claims. But if he comes forward with a valid title …

Fay How can he? He doesn't know where we are.

Sam He'd have to report it missing, of course.

Fay He can't do that. He can't say "The money I've stolen's been stolen."

Sam It may not be stolen. It could be tax evasion — in which case I have no sympathy.

Fay You haven't?

Sam No. When you think of the money I've paid in tax over the years —
money I could ill afford — it would serve the bugger right.

Fay I agree but that means it belongs to the government.

Sam Not our government, Fay. We voted Conservative.

Fay Well, what are we going to do — wait for them to get back in again?

Sam Well, it certainly won't be missed. It may seem like a lot of money to
you.

Fay Doesn't it to you?

Sam Well, yes, but not to the government: to them it's an infinitesimal drop
in the ocean — a paltry, almost laughable, amount.

Fay It's still stealing.

Sam (*sharply*) Stealing. I'm as honest as the next person ——

Fay No, you're not. I'm the next person and I want to give it back.

Sam You — honest? I don't think Sidney would agree with you. We're
trespassing. We're staying here without the owner's consent and for no
payment while I masquerade as Howard Booth — a failed actor. In
comparison with that what I'm doing is almost within the law.

Fay How?

Sam Because if we took this money to the police station and no-one claimed
it, after six months it would be ours — if the police didn't nab it first.

Fay But we haven't taken it to the police station.

Sam I can look after it just as well as the police.

Fay You mean you're going to walk around with that holdall for the rest of
the holiday?

Sam Until I've decided what to do with it — yes.

Fay sighs in exasperation and heads across the terrace to the steps

Where are you going?

Fay I'm going for a swim. I feel dirty.

Sam I'll join you.

Fay (*indicating the holdall*) What are you going to do with that? Float it on
a lilo?

Sam No. While I'm swimming you can guard it.

Fay Guard it?

Sam We'd better be vigilant, Fay — just in case …

Fay In case?

Sam That man at the airport …

Fay The smug bastard?

Sam It hadn't occurred to me before but the dark glasses, the medallion, the
expensive leisure wear — what does that say to you, Fay? It says Mafia.

Fay Mafia? Sam, what are we doing? What are we getting into?

Sam You said live dangerously.

Fay Not this dangerously.

Sam Well, at least one good thing's come out of it — we've stopped worrying about Sidney ... (*He takes a bundle of notes from the holdall and slips it into his pocket*)

Fay (*turning in astonishment*) What did you just do? You took some money.

Sam That's on account.

Fay On account of what?

Sam My silk shirts and the cashmere sweater. I think we'll go out tonight, somewhere nice; get the phrase book out, book a table for two.

Fay For two? (*She gives a withering glance at the holdall*) Don't you mean three?

Fay heads down the left-hand terrace steps and disappears from view

Sam Fay. The swimming costumes were in the blue holdall ...

Fay (*off*) That's all right. I'm living dangerously.

Fay's top flies on to the terrace, hitting Sam in the face

Sam Oh.

Sam puts Fay's top on a chair and follows her, heading for the left-hand steps. He remembers the snake just in time, reverses and goes down the right-hand steps

There is the sound of the front door opening

Howard and Dodie enter. Howard is the "smug bastard" Sam met at the airport and is dressed accordingly. He is about Sam's age and has a moustache and wears dark glasses. He is carrying a blue holdall identical to the one Sam has and has a rolled-up British newspaper under his arm. Dodie is in her twenties and attractive. She is struggling with two cases and assorted bags

Howard puts the holdall down and makes a sweeping gesture of satisfaction with the newspaper

Howard Wonderful. Spain never fails to work its magic with me, Dodie. As soon as we dropped down into Alicante and I felt that sun like the hammer blow. Wonderful. Alicante ... Even the names are more musical. Alicante, Valencia, Marbella — and what have we got? Gatwick. Which sounds strangely like an air freshener. (*He moves towards the terrace and inhales*)

Dodie Howard.

Howard Yes?

Dodie I know I had to carry my cases through the airport so that people wouldn't know we were together but we're here now … (*She glares at Howard*)

Howard Sorry, darling. I was carried away. (*He takes the cases from her*)

Dodie glares at Howard during the following

God. You're beautiful. Even after a long journey. So alert, so vital; those sudden changes of expression, those darting glances, like the sun flitting through the clouds, with the unexpected glimpse of blue skies …

Dodie continues to glare

It's the sort of beauty that makes me want to cry.

Dodie Guff.

Howard Pardon?

Dodie Guff.

Howard What do you mean — guff? I was just saying you were the most beautiful girl in the world. Is that guff?

Dodie Howard, I wasn't even the most beautiful girl on the plane. At least I didn't feel it.

Howard You were in my eyes, Dodie.

Dodie Then why didn't you sit with me?

Howard I did warn you. I told you we couldn't travel together. You saw what happened when we sat in the airport cafeteria. Everyone staring at us.

Dodie Howard, we were sitting under the bill of fare; they were looking at the prices.

Howard They were pretending to look at the prices, Dodie, but I know that stare. Heaven knows I took every precaution — I blended into the background like a chameleon. But as soon as I got onto the plane there was a buzz.

Dodie What buzz?

Howard The buzz of recognition. Of course you were back in the tail but I heard it. "Howard Booth. Howard Booth. Howard Booth."

Dodie (*sighing*) Howard, it's been twenty years since you were in "Green Acres".

Howard And I still get letters. They don't forget. When I shot myself in that covert, the nation wept. And afterwards, when they switched on their kettles, the power surge almost blew the National Grid. Surely you remember that.

Dodie I was five.

Howard Yes … You're young. You don't know the strain of living in the public eye. But if your cheese spread commercial ever takes off ——

Dodie I was recognized — by this man …

Howard (*enviously*) Were you? Obviously a cheese lover.

Dodie (*sharply*) What?

Howard But you see, it proves my point. We had to travel separately.

Dodie Not necessarily. We could have travelled as father and daughter. You've got four of them: who would know?

Howard (*shocked*) Father and daughter! Look, I know we're May and September, darling but I'm certainly not bloody January. No-one would have believed it. And if it got into the gossip columns that I was travelling to Spain with a young woman, what would Rachel say?

Dodie What would Sidney say?

Howard (*frowning*) Sidney? Why should Sidney say anything?

Dodie (*smiling*) He wanted to bring me here.

Howard Sidney? The dirty old man. At his age. I'm sorry but the thought of him running his gnarled old hands over your young body makes me shudder.

Dodie I thought he was younger than you?

Howard (*after a pause*) At the moment — yes.

Dodie What do you mean "At the moment — yes"?

Howard Well, a few years ago he was seven years younger, but on his last birthday I noticed he was only three — at the current rate I'll soon be younger than he is. I certainly look younger … (*Pause*) I said I certainly look younger.

Dodie Yes.

Howard I wish you'd say that with a little more conviction.

Dodie I don't mind you looking old. I just don't like to feel used.

Howard Are you saying that because you paid my air fare? You know I have no money.

Dodie It's not that. But you have been married three times. I feel you've said all these things before.

Howard You think it makes me insincere?

Dodie You never use one cliché where two will do.

Howard They're not clichés. I'm a romantic. All my life I've pursued the blue bird of happiness — and now I've found it.

Dodie (*grinning*) But three times. You must have had that engagement ring on a string.

Howard I consider that an extremely tasteless remark, Dodie. (*He turns away*)

Dodie I'm sorry, Howard. (*She moves closer to Howard*) Let's go for a swim.

Howard Wait until the sun goes down.

Dodie Why?

Howard I'm supposed to be in Scotland.

Dodie Scotland!

Howard Yes. I told Rachel I was going to Scotland to do a couple of days' filming, and it's only sixty-five in Edinburgh — and it's raining. A suntan would take some explaining.

Dodie What are you doing to do? Crawl under a stone for the rest of the week?

Howard No but it means I'll flit through the sun fairly quickly.

Dodie (*tartly*) Perhaps we could get you a bathing machine. (*She moves towards the door*)

Howard All right. I'm sorry. I'll risk it. I'll say I found a sunbed somewhere.

Dodie Where's the bedroom?

Howard drags the cases into the hall during the following

Howard Upstairs. The master bedroom. Sidney doesn't let everyone use it but since I'm a valued client, he gave me a key … (*He tries to unlock the holdall*) I'll get my costume … (*He stops*) Hallo …

Dodie (*pausing at the door*) What's the matter?

Howard The key doesn't fit.

Dodie Let me see.

Howard Wait a minute. I knew it! This isn't my holdall. It has a horrible stain on it. Look. I was right. It was that pipsqueak at the airport. I knew he'd taken my holdall.

Dodie Then why didn't you say something?

Howard He was so positive and I couldn't afford a scene. I think he recognized me. He had this wild look in his eye, and I thought of John Lennon … Now I've nothing to wear!

Dodie picks up the last of her cases. The blue holdall and the newspaper are now the only items left in the room that were brought in by Howard and Dodie

Well, when we've unpacked, we'll have to go back to Alicante.

Howard (*helping Dodie with the case*) Yes. It's not just the clothes; there were my priceless old videos.

Dodie (*staring*) You brought your old videos here?

Howard Yes. Sidney's got a recorder. I thought you might be interested …

Dodie My God! Howard!

Dodie exits

Howard Dodie.

Howard follows Dodie off

Fay puts her head around the pillar at the top of the steps. Sam puts his head around the pillar on the other side

Fay (*hissing*) I'm sure there's someone here. Get my clothes.

Sam, who has removed his jacket but is still holding the holdall, moves forward cautiously and picks up Fay's clothes from the chair. He tries to peer into the room

Sam I can't see anyone.

Sam hands Fay her clothes

Fay They must have gone.
Sam Probably the villa people.
Fay I'll get dressed.

   Fay disappears

Sam comes into the room. He sees the blue holdall and stares

   Howard enters from the hall and picks up his blue holdall

Sam and Howard both stand still, holding the identical holdalls. They regard each other

Sam It's you — isn't it?
Howard You recognize me?
Sam Yes, you're the smug ... You were at the airport. I took your holdall. I've been trying to find you.

Howard removes his dark glasses and stares

Howard So it's you. The pip ... the man at the carousel.
Sam Right.
Howard You took my holdall. You called me Buster.
Sam (*apologetically*) I was in a state. I've lost both my parents this year.
Howard I don't care if you've lost the whole family; there's such a thing as good manners.
Sam (*humbly*) I know, but I hate flying. Then there was the turbulence, and all those awful people, in singlets and tattoos. I thought, God, I don't want to die with this lot. You know the things that go through your head …
Howard Yes, well, I don't normally travel package but I had my reasons …
Sam (*giving a nervous thumbs-up*) I'm sure you did.
Howard What? (*He stares*) Are you sure you don't know me?
Sam (*hastily*) No. I've never seen you before in my life, but then I'm terrible with faces.

Howard Are you?

Sam If anyone asked for a description of you I couldn't give it. Nothing personal but as far as I'm concerned you have a totally forgettable face.

Howard I've never been told that before.

Sam Oh, it's not you — it's me. It's a psychological thing. There's a name for it — I can't remember that either. I'm all right on houses and streets — find my way anywhere — but not faces. My own wife.

Howard (*staring*) You don't remember her?

Sam I've often confused her with someone who works at Tesco's.

Howard Good Lord.

Sam Well, here's your holdall. I'm sorry I had to open it.

Howard You opened it?

Sam I had to find out who owned it. And you didn't put your name on it.

Howard I had my reasons for not putting my name on it.

Sam (*winking*) I'm sure you did. But if you had put your name on it, Mr …?

Howard Smith.

Sam Smith — of course. (*He gives the thumbs-up again*) And your address … I wouldn't have had to open it, would I?

Howard Your name wasn't on either but I didn't force my way into your bag. I locked my holdall because the contents were of considerable value …

Sam (*with another wink*) You're telling me. (*Hastily*) Not that it's any of my business.

Howard I think I'd better check the contents, Mr … (*He moves towards the holdall*)

Sam Booth.

Howard (*turning*) Booth?

Sam Howard Booth?

Howard That name seems strangely familiar.

Sam You may know me better as Seth Warren.

Howard The gamekeeper in "Green Acres" — the one who shot himself?

Sam The same.

Howard I thought you were taller.

Sam rises on the balls of his feet

Sam Everyone says that. That's because I used to move around on the balls of my feet — gives the illusion of height.

Howard Really?

Sam It's an old acting trick. And of course the rest of the cast were extremely short.

Howard I didn't know that.

Sam They were noted for it. They were the shortest cast of any long running soap.

Howard What about Big Jim Strudwick?

Sam Big Jim Strudwick?

Howard The landlord of the *Swan*. Giant of a man.

Sam Five foot six.

Howard No. But he towered over that bar.

Sam Stood on a box.

Howard What about when he walked around the bar?

Sam We all crouched slightly.

Howard Fascinating. I must say I love these glimpses behind the scenes. I can't get over how much you've changed. I know what it is: you've shaved off your moustache.

Sam I always do that for the holidays, so that I'm not recognized. Not that there's much chance of that these days.

Howard Oh, I think people still remember you. I thought you were very good in "Green Acres".

Sam No, I was tripe.

Howard (*shocked*) Tripe.

Sam That's why they wrote me out.

Howard I thought it was a vendetta.

Sam No – tripe.

Howard (*coldly*) I think you're being extremely modest but then I must say you seem totally lacking in theatricality. You could be almost anyone.

Sam I am on holiday — love.

Howard Is your wife with you?

Sam Yes.

Howard Rachel Kent! How exciting. I'm dying to meet her.

Sam She's changed too.

Howard Has she?

Sam And she looks much shorter.

Howard But she still has the flaming red hair?

Sam What?

Howard The flaming red hair.

Sam It has faded — with the sun …

Howard You do surprise me. (*He picks up Sam's holdall*) But then life's full of surprises. Would it surprise you to know my name's Howard too … ?

Sam Really?

Howard In fact my name happens to be Howard —— (*He looks into the holdall. He stares at the money. His mouth drops open. He stares wildly at Sam and back at the money. He swallows*) — Smith …

Sam Yes. You said. I hope it's all in order?

Howard Yes. (*He breathes heavily*) It seems perfectly in order.

Sam I — er — borrowed a few pounds — out-of-pocket expenses.

Howard Keep it. You deserve it. One doesn't often come across such honesty. I'm moved. Here, take some more.

Howard gives Sam a bundle of money

And I hope you have a wonderful holiday, Mr Booth — you've certainly made mine.

Howard guides Sam towards the door

Sam Thank you.
Howard No, thank you and goodbye.
Sam Goodbye.

They both stand by the door waiting for the other to leave

Howard Was there anything else?
Sam I don't think so.
Howard (*cautiously*) Perhaps a drink?
Sam Why not? (*He moves towards the kitchen*)
Howard I'll get it. Gin and tonic?

Howard exits with the holdall

Sam looks slightly perplexed

Fay enters

Fay Has he gone?
Sam No — he's in the kitchen.
Fay What's he doing in there?
Sam Mixing drinks. He's taken the place over, Fay.
Fay Who is he?
Sam It's the Mafia.
Fay What!
Sam He's come for his money.
Fay My God! I knew he'd find us. What's he like?
Sam Silky — and smooth, but there's the smell of the prison yard about him, Fay. I wouldn't like to cross him.
Fay Did he mind about the money?
Sam No — he just seemed pleased to get it back.
Fay Then why hasn't he gone? Why is he in there making drinks? He could be working up to something …
Sam What?
Fay Violence.
Sam No — he seemed perfectly happy.

Fay But what about when we get home? He could be measuring us up for concrete overcoats.

Sam No — I boxed clever. I told him I was Howard Booth. And the villa people will confirm that. So if he takes a contract out on anyone it's going to be Howard Booth — and according to you it won't be the first time he's died a death.

Fay But you're nothing like Howard Booth.

Sam Well, you're nothing like Rachel Kent.

Fay (*staring*) Rachel Kent?

Sam His wife. And if you think Howard Booth's tricky — she's got flaming red hair.

Fay (*appalled*) You told him I was Rachel Kent? But she's well-known — she's never off the box. And she's got flaming red hair.

Sam I said it had faded. Just don't let him get too close.

Fay (*turning*) I'll go in the garden.

Sam No, he wants to meet you. He'll have one drink and go. You'll get away with it.

Fay But Rachel Kent is incredibly beautiful.

Sam Is she? That's going to make it difficult … (*He moves to the terrace*) I know … (*He rummages around in the beach bag. He finds a bathing hat and a snorkel mask*) Put these on. We'll say you've been practising snorkelling in the pool — and you're getting used to the mask …

Fay puts on the snorkel and mask

What do you think … ?

Fay She also has the most incredible legs.

Sam Oh dear. More trouble. I know — put these flippers on …

Sam pulls a pair of flippers from the bag and helps Fay on with them

Fay Why the flippers?

Sam It'll take his mind off your legs.

Fay (*flapping across the room; nervously*) How do I look?

Sam Fine. Just try and look a little more theatrical.

Fay How can I be theatrical in flippers?

Dodie enters from the hall. She stares in surprise at Sam

Sam Hallo …

Dodie Hallo.

Sam Are you with Howard?

Dodie Yes.

Sam I'm Howard too. This is Rachel. Rachel Kent.

Dodie sees Fay for the first time

Dodie Oh, my God!

Sam Don't be alarmed. Rachel has been practising her snorkelling. She wants to get the feel of the mask.

Fay (*muffled*) Hallo, darling … (*She flaps towards Dodie*)

Dodie (*backing away*) Rachel. What must you think of me?

Fay Pardon?

Dodie I can't make any excuse for what I've done. I can't explain it. Perhaps if I'd met you before all this happened … (*She stops*) I thought you were taller.

Fay I used to be. It's married life I'm afraid.

Dodie Yes, I know how you must feel. And I'm so sorry. I can't excuse what I've done — I can't explain it. I didn't mean it to happen.

Fay I'm sure you didn't. He led you on I suppose.

Dodie Yes. It was all his idea.

Fay (*with a glance at Sam*) That's the trouble with men — they can't keep their hands off anything.

Dodie Say you forgive me, Rachel.

Fay Well, it's not for me to say ——

Dodie (*seizing Fay's hand*) Please.

Sam (*whispering*) Forgive her.

Fay I forgive you.

Dodie kisses Fay's hand

The blue holdall is thrown into the room. They stare at it

> *Howard follows the holdall on, carrying two plastic goblets on a tray and holding a bottle in the other hand*

Dodie Howard. Did you know Rachel was here?

Howard What! (*He drops the tray and just manages to hold on to the bottle*) Where?

Dodie (*pointing at Fay*) There.

Howard (*staring at Fay as if she is odd*) No — that's not Rachel. Rachel's taller and with much better legs.

Dodie But she says she's Rachel Kent.

Howard That's nothing; he says he's Howard Booth.

Dodie Why?

Howard God knows. Delusions of grandeur, I suppose. It doesn't matter; they're just leaving.

Sam Who's leaving?

Howard You are. I don't know what you're doing masquerading as Howard
   Booth but ——

Sam How do you know I'm not Howard Booth?

Howard Because I am.

Sam Oh. Then what were you doing masquerading as Howard Smith?

Howard That's my business.

Sam It wouldn't have anything to do with the money, I suppose?

Dodie What money?

Howard As a matter of fact it's because I wish to avoid the attentions of the
   media.

Sam What media? I don't see any around here.

Howard That's because I call myself Smith. (*He pauses, studying Sam and
   Fay*) I know what you're doing here. You're trespassing — you're
   interlopers.

Sam and Fay look uneasy

That's why you called yourself Booth. You thought I wasn't coming. Do
   you know they've even begun to eat their way through the starter pack,
   Dodie?

Sam I thought your wife's name was Rachel?

Howard It is.

Sam So that's why you called yourself Smith.

Howard Would you kindly get your things and leave?

Sam And leave you with the money I suppose.

Dodie What money? What's he talking about, Howard?

Sam I'm talking about half a million in that holdall.

Dodie looks into the holdall and gasps

Dodie I don't believe it. And I had to pay for his plane ticket.

Sam (*suspiciously*) What?

Dodie How did you come by this money, Howard? You were supposed to
   be broke.

Sam Yes, tell us.

Howard (*after a pause*) How did I come by it? (*Slowly*) Suppose I said I
   saved it over the years — secretly, from my predatory wives …

Fay (*removing the mask*) Saved it. You haven't earned a penny in years. The
   last time you were on television you were wearing flares.

Howard (*staring*) My God! I know you — you work in the office.

Fay Yes. (*Significantly*) I keep the books.

Howard Ah. (*More slowly*) Suppose I said it didn't go through the books.
   Suppose I said it was from personal appearances — opening supermarkets,
   et cetera.

Dodie Opening supermarkets. The only thing you've opened recently is a giro.

Fay This money isn't yours, is it?

Howard I only said suppose. And talking about "suppose" — you're not supposed to be here. What would Sidney say?

Fay If it comes to that, what would Rachel say?

Dodie If this is your holdall, Howard, where are your old videos?

Howard Well, it looked like my holdall.

Sam It looked like my holdall but that's not the point. You were going to take the money, weren't you?

Fay, Sam and Dodie look at Howard accusingly

Howard Not really … Look, I'm as honest as the next man.

Fay I'd check who you're standing next to before you say that.

Howard After all, it's my holdall that's missing — I'm merely hanging on to this until I get mine back.

Fay That's what Sam said.

Howard There you are then — he's got his back, now it's my turn.

Dodie Shouldn't we take it to the police?

Fay That's what I said.

Howard That is an alternative but we are in a grey area here …

Sam That's what I said.

Fay What grey area?

Howard We don't know where the money comes from or where it's going …

Fay I think I know where it's going …

Howard This is probably the proceeds from international crime — probably going to be laundered — or used for drugs. We could be returning this only to fuel more human misery.

Sam That's right.

Howard Perhaps we were meant to find the money. (*He pauses and looks upward*) Perhaps He intended it …

Sam You mean — God?

Fay You're not bringing God into it?

Howard Why not? Would we do so much harm with it? Why is it that the wrong people always have the money? Because they lie and cheat. Don't you ever want to say: "Enough is enough? Why not me for a change?"

Sam And me.

Howard I have a son with a drink problem, another one on drugs; don't you think I want to help them?

Sam I have one with learning difficulties.

Howard There you are, you see. (*Pause*) And I suppose — and I'm talking hypothetically here — that a hundred thousand of this, Sam, would make a considerable difference to your life?

Sam (*after a pause*) I think two hundred and fifty thousand would make a bigger difference …

Howard You mean half?

Sam Talking hypothetically.

Howard Well — talking hypothetically — isn't that rather greedy? After all, it is my holdall that's missing. I thought I was being generous. I mean, I'm the only person with any claim to the money.

Sam I found it.

Fay I think we should take it to the police station.

Sam (*sharply*) Take those flippers off, Fay — you look ridiculous.

Fay sheepishly removes the flippers

Howard And if we took it to the police station where would it get us?

Sam Precisely. A few weeks ago I found an old age pensioner's wallet in the street. It was crammed with notes; I'd never seen so much money in a wallet.

Howard They do awfully well — pensioners.

Sam It was the end of the month and I was broke but I took it back to his house. He was going out of his mind, his hand trembled when I gave it to him, there were tears in his eyes — and do you know something: the old skinflint didn't even give me a penny towards the petrol.

Howard Very mean — pensioners.

Fay But you didn't do it for that, Sam. Didn't you feel good?

Sam No.

Howard I know how Sam feels. Pensioners have never been better off — they've never had it so good. But who cares about the forties-to-fifties?

Dodie (*surprised*) Forties-to-fifties?

Howard As the Bard said "Who would fardels bear to grunt and sweat under a weary life" if he could do something about it. Hey, Sam?

Sam Well, I don't know what fardels are but I've certainly grunted and sweated under a weary life. And I'm not settling for anything less than fifty-fifty. (*Pause*) Talking hypothetically.

Fay I still think we should take it to the police station.

Sam Fay, you're beginning to sound like a bloody parrot.

Howard Fay, if we did that we might never see it again.

Fay Why should we see it again?

Sam Howard means it may fall into the wrong hands.

Dodie I think it already has.

Howard All right, Sam. Straight down the middle. Fifty-fifty.

Howard and Sam shake hands solemnly

Dodie (*after a pause. Quietly*) What about me?

Howard (*politely*) Sorry, Dodie. What was that?

Dodie What about me?

Howard You? Well, when I said fifty-fifty I assumed I was speaking for you as well, Dodie.

Dodie Well, you weren't. After all, if I hadn't paid for your flight you wouldn't have been here.

Howard Ah, quite right; you want paying for the tickets …

Dodie No, I want my share.

Howard Share?

Dodie I want what you're getting.

Howard But, Dodie — I was going to share it with you.

Dodie Were you?

Howard (*frowning*) Dodie, are you suggesting a three-way split?

Dodie That's right.

Howard I see. I'm sorry, Dodie, that was presumptuous of me. You're right. You can see her point of view, Sam. It means a third each.

Sam What do you mean — a third each?

Howard Three people — a third each.

Sam What about Fay?

Fay What?

Howard Ah, but Fay's your wife; that makes you a legal entity and in these circumstances you're treated as one.

Sam We're not one. Fay's a person in her own right.

Fay Thank you. And I think we should take it back to ——

Howard Be reasonable, Sam. After all, it's not as if I'm asking for anything for my wife, is it?

Sam (*aghast*) Your wife! She's not even here.

Howard No, but if she were here she'd certainly want her share — whereas your wife wishes to take it to the police station.

Sam I don't care what she wants to do. I'm speaking on her behalf.

Howard You can't. She's an individual in her own right. You just said so.

Sam I don't care what I said — if your girlfriend gets a share, so does my wife.

Howard All right. Twenty-five per cent each. There's no point in arguing about it. And we are talking hypothetically. After all, we don't even know where this money came from …

Dodie (*quietly*) I think I do … (*She picks up the crumpled newspaper*) I read it on the plane … Listen. (*She reads*) "Daring raid on the North Circular. Armoured van hit by ram-raiders on its way to the Mint."

Fay Oh, no!

Dodie (*reading*) "The attack was particularly brutal. Ammonia was thrown into the guard's face — and the driver was stuck to his steering wheel with Superglue."

Fay That Superglue's terrible.

Dodie (*reading*) "The driver had to be cut from his cab and the steering wheel removed in surgery."

Fay Now perhaps you realize who you're dealing with.

Dodie There's more. (*She reads*) "Acting on a tip-off the police raided a house in South London last night. In the shoot-out that followed ——"

Fay Shoot out!

Dodie " — two of the gang were killed and three policemen wounded. One of the gang is rumoured to have escaped, and a considerable sum of money in used notes is still unaccounted for … "

Howard (*picking up the blue holdall*) So that's it. I think I'd better put this in a safe place …

Sam Do you mean, hide it?

Howard Well, yes.

Sam Why should *you* hide it?

Howard Don't you trust me?

Sam I just don't like the way you've assumed responsibility for it. Why don't we both hide it?

Howard I should have thought that was obvious: the fewer people who know where the money is, the better.

Sam All right. I'll hide it. (*He takes a grip on the holdall*)

Howard You're not thinking, Sam. The ruthless thug who stole this money must have been at Alicante. He probably didn't come forward for his holdall because he was being watched. He may have even seen you take it …

Sam gradually releases his hold on the holdall during the following

He may follow you here. If he does — you'll be able to deny all knowledge of the money …

Sam What about you?

Howard I shall dissemble.

Sam Dissemble?

Howard I'm an actor, Sam. It's my line of work.

Fay He's right, Sam.

Howard Of course I'm right.

The doorbell rings

Howard (*with a start*) My God! What was that?

Dodie It was the front door.

Fay It's probably him.

Howard (*fearfully*) You think so?

Sam Well?

Howard What?

Sam Aren't you going to dissemble?

Howard You'd better go and see who it is, Dodie.

Dodie I'm not going on my own …

Howard Right … But don't leave me, no matter what happens. I find a woman is a calming influence in these situations … (*He slips the holdall into a cupboard*)

Dodie exits; Howard follows her

Sam and Fay look around for somewhere to hide. Sam takes the large straw sombrero from the stand on the terrace and pulls it on in attempt to disguise himself

Fay listens at the door

Fay It's all right. It's a woman.

Sam joins Fay and listens. The sound of a conversation, the words indistinct, between Howard, Dodie and an Englishwoman, can be heard during the following

Sam It's the woman from the villa below. (*He listens again*) She's come for an autograph.

Fay She'll wonder how he's managed to grow a moustache in half an hour.

Sam She didn't get a good look at me — I was standing with the sun at my back.

Fay I think you stood in it too long. I think you've got heatstroke. This money's going to cause nothing but trouble.

Sam Why should it? Howard was right about one thing — it's the wrong people who have the money … Unfortunately he's one of them. Did you notice his eyes when he looked at the money? They were like the keys of a cash register. Have you ever seen a look like that before?

Fay (*regarding Sam*) Only once … .

Sam I don't trust him. A few minutes ago he was ready to go off with the money without a word … (*He takes the holdall from the cupboard*)

Fay What are you doing?

Sam I'm switching the holdalls. (*He exchanges the holdalls and puts the holdall with the money behind the settee*)

Fay But you can't.

Sam Only temporarily — until we find out what's what.

Fay And what happens when we find out what's what?

Sam We'll cross that bridge when we come to it.

Fay Don't you think you're being mean?

Sam Mean? An hour ago I was worth half a million: now it's a hundred and twenty-five thousand! I don't call that mean.

Fay Sam, this morning you were worth a hundred and fifty pounds – just try and remember that.

Sam Yes, I was worth a hundred and fifty pounds and I bought my suits from Oxfam. I wear dead men's clothes, Fay. Widows burst into tears when they meet me in the street. Well, all that's going to change.

Fay You keep talking about this money as if it's yours: it isn't. It's tainted. Men have died for this money.

Sam It's not tainted, Fay. It's as good or as bad as the person who has it. Do you know where this money was going, Fay?

Fay To the Mint.

Sam To a fire. It was going up in smoke. They were going to burn it.

Fay Burn it?

Sam What good would that have done? Would that have helped our children? Would that have helped your mother?

Fay (*amazed*) My mother? You were going to help my mother?

Sam I know we've had our differences but it couldn't have been easy for her since your father died. I intended to give her a few thousand …

Fay Oh, Sam.

Sam And the children. Have you thought about the children during all this?

Fay Well, no …

Sam (*shaking his head*) Some mother.

Fay But it's not ours.

Sam But if it were?

Fay Then there could be special tuition for Tim — and Sue could go to college …

Sam Yes, but I was thinking more of improving the quality of their lives. Have you looked at that bathroom recently?

Fay Bathroom?

Sam We need a decent bathroom, Fay. With sepia tinted mirrors, diffused lighting, bidet and a sunken bath.

Fay Sam, there's no room for a bidet, even if you knew how to use one. And a sunken bath would poke through the ceiling.

Sam Fay, I'm not talking about our bathroom. I wouldn't stay there. You have such narrow horizons.

Fay (*excitedly*) Sam, you don't mean *The Limes*? That's always been our dream.

Sam *The Limes*.

Fay It's up for sale again.

Sam (*scornfully*) *The Limes*. Two recep., kitch. and conserv. Where's the room for a study?

Fay You don't study.

Sam I've never had the room. And where would we put the bar?

Fay What's wrong with the sideboard?

Sam Everything. You're so provincial. And another thing — those limes.

Fay They're beautiful; so cool in summer.

Sam Any idea what they'd do to the bodywork of a decent car when they shed their flowers?

Fay You haven't got a decent car.

Sam I will have.

Fay I should have thought a home came before a car.

Sam I'm not buying *The Limes* and that's final.

Fay Well, I may have something to say about that ... (*She stops*) What am I talking about? It's not our money.

Sam (*listening*) She's leaving. Don't say anything.

Fay He'll guess. I'll look flustered, you know I will.

Sam Then don't meet his eye. Do what you always do — look in your handbag.

Howard and Dodie enter looking pleased

Fay dives into her handbag

Howard Autograph hunters; it never ends.

Dodie She even asked for mine.

Howard Yes, another cheese lover — apparently. (*He gives a reproachful glance at Sam*) Incidentally, she thought I looked much more like Howard Booth close to. (*He takes Sam's holdall from the cupboard*) Well, I'd better put this in a safe place ...

Fay directs her gaze at the floor

(*Staring curiously at Fay*) Have you lost something, Fay?

Fay No, I don't think so ...

Howard Do you want to come with me, Sam, see where I put it?

Sam No ... I suppose we've got to start trusting each other sometime.

Howard Yes ... (*He studies Sam*) Still, I suppose we'd better count the money so that we all know just how much there is.

Sam (*quickly*) I wouldn't. Not now. I thought I saw someone out there. A big ugly brute ...

Howard Really? Are you sure?

Howard moves to the terrace, carrying the holdall

Raynor enters. He is a powerfully built man in his thirties with battered features and an air of menace. He is carrying a blue holdall identical to the other two

Sam looks as surprised as anyone

Howard drops his holdall behind him

They all regard each other

Raynor Your name Booth, guvnor?
Howard Yes.
Raynor I thought so. My name's Raynor. I came in through the garden gate. I hope you don't mind …
Howard (*hastily*) Not at all. You want to use the garden gate — use the garden gate …

Raynor looks around narrowly

Dodie stands motionless

Fay suddenly takes out a handkerchief and uses it as a duster, flicking away at the furniture and muttering to herself in Spanish. Sam takes her cue, pulls the straw hat over his eyes, finds the brush on the terrace and begins sweeping

Raynor gazes suspiciously at Sam

Sam (*heavy accent*) Ole. Muchos Grossos.
Raynor (*uncertainly*) Yes …
Howard Can I help you?
Raynor Yeh. (*He dumps his holdall in front of Howard*) I've got a problem, John. Perhaps you can help. Wait a minute. Don't I know you?
Howard (*modestly*) I'm afraid so. Price of fame I suppose …
Raynor No, not you, John — the lady … (*He moves to Dodie*) Where have I seen you before … ?
Howard Do you like cheese?
Dodie I do the cheese spread commercial.
Raynor Of course. The cheese spread commercial. I should have known, you're terrific. The way you spread that cheese — and moisten your lips and say ——
Dodie (*pouting*) "Gorgeous."
Raynor Yeh, terrific.
Dodie I have worked on it.

Howard Yes … I've always refused to do them myself – though I can see the advantages. Although whether an actor really wants to be associated with cheese I'm not sure …

Dodie (*quietly*) Better than ham.

Raynor Now, this is the problem, John. I seem to have picked your holdall up from the airport …

Howard My holdall?

Raynor Yes. And since I've picked up your holdall I have to assume that you picked up mine …

Howard Picked up yours?

Raynor I'm referring to that holdall behind you.

Howard This holdall? (*He gives the holdall a startled glance as if he's never seen it before*)

Raynor Yes, that holdall.

Howard Is this holdall yours?

Raynor It seems a fair assumption.

Howard You mean there's been some sort of mistake?

Raynor At the airport. My fault entirely. I do apologize.

Howard Not at all. I should have checked. But as you see I've just arrived. I didn't realize I had the wrong holdall.

Raynor So, it hasn't been tampered with … ?

Howard Well, I can't vouch that it hasn't been tampered with. But I certainly haven't tampered with it — I'm not the tampering type. Why don't you check?

Raynor Why don't I?

Fay gasps and looks up from her dusting. Raynor looks at her thoughtfully

Fay (*brightly*) Encantado.

Raynor Yeh … (*He examines the holdall*) Well, it doesn't look as if it's been tampered with … I'm afraid I had to open yours …

Howard That's all right. You had to find out who I was … (*He hopes for recognition*) And now you know — Howard Booth …

Raynor Yeh, your car rental details were in the holdall.

Howard Oh.

Raynor Look, John, I'm sorry if I made that tasteless remark about tampering ——

Howard My name's Howard. (*Prompting*) Howard Booth.

Raynor Yeh. I'm afraid I have a suspicious nature. My friends often complain about it.

Howard No, I can understand — it's the parts I have to play: good-looking, slightly dodgy, emotionally cold. You're bound to be confused.

Raynor Are you an actor then?

Howard Of course I'm an actor. I was Seth Warren in "Green Acres".
Raynor Seth Warren? With the sideboards and the droopy moustache?
Howard Yes. I shot myself in a covert.
Raynor Yeh, I remember. Why did you do that?
Howard It was remorse — after killing the poacher.
Raynor I wouldn't have done it.
Howard Well, I wouldn't have done it if I'd had any choice. It was a vendetta.
   I quarrelled with the writers over dinner. Someone had an extra pudding
   and they said it was me. Then they got drunk and started shouting "In the
   beginning was the word" and I told them they couldn't write a note for the
   milkman. A few weeks later I was shooting myself in a covert.
Raynor I'm sorry — I didn't realize I was talking to somebody famous. I
   hope you don't think I was out of order.
Howard Not at all. And if you're worried about the contents of your holdall
   I suggest you check them now, so there's no misunderstanding …
Raynor (*uneasily*) No, that's all right.
Howard No, I insist. I wouldn't like to be accused of taking anything …

Raynor hesitates

Fay drops a vase

Fay Oh, *negligente*!

*Sam appears at the door and leans on his brush. He abuses Fay in bogus
Spanish. He achieves fluency by putting os after almost every word*

Sam Matos batitos grossos! Eh. Muchacos tattos. Patatos fritos! Cuando —
   cuando — cuando.
Fay Si.
Sam Colosos — cassos! Tomatos prossos. Eh. Encantados denados muchos?
   Litros passasos. Eh. La cuenta muchos – vamoosos.
Fay Si.
Sam (*concluding the argument*) Grossos muchos. (*Bitterly*) Bassos.
Raynor Well, I won't disturb you … any further… I can see you have a
   domestic crisis on your hands …
Howard (*indicating the exit to the front door*) This way …
Raynor (*furtively*) No. I'll leave by the garden gate. I have this superstition
   — about leaving by the same door …
Raynor Have a nice holiday. Goodbye …
Howard (*regretfully*) Goodbye, Mr Raynor.

Raynor moves on to the terrace with his holdall. He looks curiously at Sam

   Bye.

Sam (*coldly*) Bueno.

Raynor exits

Howard, Sam, Dodie and Fay breathe a sigh of relief

Howard (*apologetically*) I'm sorry — but what else could I do?
Sam You did the right thing, Howard. Our personal safety comes first.
Dodie We didn't want sticking together with Superglue.
Howard But when I think of all that money ...
Sam Well, it was never really ours, was it?
Howard I suppose not.
Sam And what you've never had you won't miss. Fay, we'd better get those
   cases packed ...
Howard (*surprised*) You're leaving?
Sam We can't stay here — it wouldn't be fair.
Dodie There's no hurry.
Sam We'd like to get fixed up in Javea ... Give me a hand with the cases,
   Fay.
Fay Yes, of course.

Fay exits, keeping her gaze on the floor. Sam follows

Howard I must say he's taken it very well.
Dodie Did you notice the way she looked at the floor all the time?
Howard Probably contemplating a little hoovering.
Dodie I think she was hiding something. And what about the holdall? The
   holdall Raynor took away was locked. The holdall with the money in had
   been forced open.
Howard You're right! He switched the holdalls! Of all the dirty tricks. How
   can anyone sink so low? (*He looks around the room and discovers the
   holdall behind the settee*) And here it is!
Dodie What are we going to do?
Howard Switch them back again. (*He takes his holdall from the middle of
   the floor and switches it with the holdall behind the settee*)
Dodie Quickly, he's coming back.

Sam enters, his arms full of holdalls and cases, clearly in a hurry

Howard (*smiling*) Can we give you a hand?
Sam Thanks.

Dodie and Howard help Sam with the cases; they head for the hall

Dodie (*indicating the holdall behind the settee*) There's a holdall behind
   here.
Sam (*quickly*) No, leave that. Fay wants to put one or two things in it …

Howard and Dodie exchange glances

They all exit into the hall

There are the sounds of doors opening and closing, off

   Fay enters. She moves towards the holdall behind the settee, then hesitates

   Sam puts his head around the door

Sam (*hissing*) Bring the holdall, Fay.
Fay Where are they?
Sam (*smiling*) Helping me to load the car. They don't suspect a thing …
Fay Can't we just forget it?
Sam Forget it. Half a million. Are you mad?
Fay But he'll come back for it.
Sam We won't be here — we'll be in Madrid.
Fay He's a desperate man, Sam.
Sam Not as desperate as I am. You'd better hang on to my coat tails, Fay.
   We're going all the way. Now bring that holdall. I'll get the car started …

   Sam exits

*Fay looks desperate. She hesitates, then switches the holdalls back again,
believing that she is now leaving the money behind. She moves to the door.
As she does so:*

   Sam bursts in breathlessly

Sam Quick! Take the holdall out the back and hide it.
Fay What's the matter?
Sam It's Raynor. He's in a car at the bottom of the drive.
Fay We'll have to give it to him.
Sam Why? He doesn't know we've got it. He can't be sure. Now hide it!
   Quickly!

   Fay exits into the garden

   Howard and Dodie enter

Howard Funny. Raynor's back — I wonder why … ?

Sam You seem amused.

Howard Yes, it's all this excitement. It's made me quite hysterical … (*He picks up his holdall*) Well, Dodie, should we go and settle in?

Howard and Dodie exit, smiling

Sam stares after them suspiciously

Fay returns from the garden

Sam Did you hide it?

Fay Yes. Why is he sitting in the car? Why doesn't he come in?

Sam Because he's a fugitive. He thinks we may go to the police. He'll wait until dark. But we won't be here. (*Pause*) Why were they laughing?

Fay Who?

Sam Howard and Dodie.

Fay I don't know.

Sam They were alone with the holdall. I think I'd better check it.

Fay That's not necessary, Sam — I'm sure it's all there.

Sam You're sure? I want to be certain. Where did you hide the holdall?

Fay Leave it, Sam.

Sam takes her by the shoulders

Sam Where did you hide it?

Fay In the bougainvillaea — at the foot of the steps — on the *left-hand* side.

Sam (*staring*) What?

Fay hisses like a snake and exits

CURTAIN

ACT II

Scene 1

The villa. A few minutes later

When the Curtain *opens, Sam is on the terrace. He is looking anxiously down the steps to where he saw the snake*

Fay enters from the hall

Sam (*moving to meet Fay*) Is he still there?

Fay Yes. He's sitting in his car looking thoughtful. No doubt wondering how he's become the proud possessor of a couple of silk shirts, a cashmere sweater, and a bottle of Givenchy for Men.

Sam Well, we don't have to explain. Let's get the holdall and make our way across the gardens. We can leave the rest of the luggage; we won't need it.

Fay I've got a better idea — let's take the rest of the luggage and leave the holdall.

Sam No — I want that holdall, Fay.

Fay Then get it.

Sam You know I can't do that. You know I'm terrified of snakes. If I see it I'll have a stroke and they'll get the money.

Fay Well, at least you'll die honest.

Howard enters, followed by Dodie

Howard (*angrily*) All right. Where's the money, Sam?

Fay (*puzzled*) What?

Sam (*innocently*) I thought you gave it to Raynor.

Howard No — *I* thought I gave it to Raynor. But you switched the holdalls.

Sam What makes you think that?

Dodie Because Raynor's still out there.

Howard Yes. Now, I switched the holdalls back again and ——

Fay Wait a minute. You switched the holdalls?

Howard Yes.

Sam Are you talking about my holdall or Raynor's holdall?

Howard (*confused*) What?

Sam I mean which one did you switch for your holdall? Or was it your holdall you switched for one of them.

Howard (*staring wildly*) What?

Fay Howard, did you switch the holdall after you thought someone had switched the holdall or did you switch the holdall before you thought someone had switched the holdall?

Howard I don't know! All I know is that when I came to check my holdall ——

Sam So you have got your holdall?

Howard Yes!

Sam Just checking.

Howard When I came to check my holdall I found my clothes and a few videos.

Sam Well, you would if it was your holdall.

Howard I know!

Sam Then what are you complaining about? At least you've got your videos.

Howard I didn't want the videos!

Dodie And he doesn't say that lightly.

Howard Dodie, can we dispense with the verbal sniping for a moment? I'm trying to explain.

Dodie Then why don't you simply say that the holdall that Raynor took was locked whereas the holdall with the money in had been forced and since we haven't got it, they must have it.

Howard (*after a pause*) I was going to say that. Now, where is it?

Sam (*after a pause*) Fay's hidden it.

Howard Where?

Sam I don't know. She wouldn't tell me.

Howard (*suspiciously*) Are you sure? I thought there were no secrets between man and wife.

Sam If there are no secrets between man and wife what are you two doing here?

Howard All right. Why don't you tell us, Fay?

Fay Because the fewer people who know where the money is the better.

Sam But we're still going to share it with you, Howard.

Howard All right, we'll deal with that later. Let's take one problem at a time. First, there's Raynor. He's a thug but he's on his own. There are four of us and one of him.

Fay Perhaps he's got accomplices.

Howard I don't think so. The rest of the gang have been caught or killed. There was a tip-off. And who had the most to gain from the tip-off? Our friend Raynor.

Sam So you think he shopped them and took the money?

Howard Yes, that means he's on his own, Sam — eliminate him and there's nothing else to worry about …

Fay (*sarcastically*) Well, that's it then, the solution's staring us in the face — why don't we simply kill him?

Howard It would be a solution.
Sam I was thinking the same thing …
Dodie It would have to look like an accident.
Howard Of course.
Fay (*staring in astonishment*) We are talking hypothetically?
Howard Hypothetically?
Fay I was joking.
Howard Murder's no joke, Fay.
Fay Well, I'm not exactly falling about.
Howard And it's not easy.
Fay How do you know? Have you done it?
Howard Yes.

There is total silence from the others

Fay (*staring*) When?
Howard Oh, several times — and I always got caught.
Dodie (*sighing*) Howard, we're not talking about acting. We're talking about real life and you only get one take.
Howard I know but it does mean I have a great deal of experience in the genre. I once played a psychopathic serial killer — I laughed as I strangled my victims …
Dodie You must have been good in it.
Howard Didn't you see it?
Dodie No, I was going to bed at seven in those days.
Howard (*frowning*) You know, what I like most about you, Dodie is the unaffected way you wear youth's proud livery. Now, where was I?
Fay Discussing murder! I can't believe this. That you're discussing killing a fellow human being.
Sam A *worthless* fellow human being, Fay.
Howard Sam's right. And after all, you raised it in the first place.

Fay gets up and moves to the hall door

Sam Where are you going?
Fay To get some fresh air.
Howard Good. Keep an eye on Raynor. He could be dangerous.
Fay *He* could be dangerous! My God!

Fay slams out of the room

Howard I hope you don't mind me saying this, Sam, but your wife's not really in the holiday mood, is she?
Sam I don't think she likes the idea, Howard.

Howard She's forgetting. That man's already responsible for two deaths. It would be natural justice, Sam.

Dodie (*thoughtfully*) Perhaps we could persuade him to take a bath …

Howard Why?

Dodie Then when he was soaking we could throw an electric fire into the water.

Howard What would that do?

Dodie Electrocute him.

Howard Ah. You mean plugged in?

Dodie Yes.

Sam It wouldn't work. It's a hundred and ten volts — it would only give him a shock.

Howard That's no good. The last thing we want to do is antagonize him.

Dodie I've got some strong sleeping tablets …

Howard (*staring*) You brought sleeping tablets here … ?

Dodie Yes. Why?

Howard Nothing. Go on.

Dodie Well. I could make a sangria and drop them in. Then we could take him for a ride and stage an accident. Hit and run.

Sam You mean run the car over him …

Dodie Yes.

Howard One snag there. Who's going to drive the car? You see whoever drives the car over our friend becomes the murderer and puts himself in the hands of the others …

Sam (*considering*) Perhaps one of us could drive while the other worked the pedals?

Howard Too difficult. We'd be lucky to hit him. Probably end up in a ditch.

Sam Then why not drug him and throw him in the pool? That way we could take an arm or a leg each. Then we'd all be involved.

Howard Wait a minute: a well-known criminal, on the run, with a fortune in used notes, happens to drown himself in our swimming pool? That would pose more problems than it solved.

Dodie Well, why don't we drown him and dump him somewhere? There's a refuse tip down the road.

Howard A refuse tip. A man found drowned in a refuse tip? Is that likely?

Sam We could dump him in the sea.

Howard There'd be no salt water in his lungs. I was caught like that once.

Dodie What about a fall from the bedroom balcony? Drug him and drop him off.

Howard It's only a few feet. It might not work.

Dodie We could keep doing it until it does.

Howard (*appalled*) Keep doing it until it does! We can't keep dropping him off the balcony. What would the neighbours say? Besides, we'd still have to get rid of the body.

Dodie I know. Drug him, drown him in the pool, take him out — and run the car over him.

Howard A drowned man walks in front of a car ... Is that the same man who drowned in a refuse tip? Don't be ridiculous, Dodie.

Dodie They wouldn't know he was drowned because we'd have squashed the water out of him.

Howard Squashed the water out of him. That's bizarre.

Dodie All you do is make objections.

Howard I'm trying to be logical.

Sam Look, let's drug him first and then make a decision.

Fay enters

Fay He's not in the car.

Sam Where is he?

Fay I don't know.

Sam We told you to watch him.

Fay I did. He was there one moment — the next moment he was gone.

Howard Dodie, perhaps this is the time to make the sangria.

Dodie exits

He may be armed, Sam. We'll need something heavy. Is that a croquet mallet out on the terrace ... ?

Sam Yes.

Howard drifts casually out on to the terrace and selects a croquet mallet

Fay Sam, you're not serious about this?

Sam Fay, I've waited all my life for this opportunity. I'm not letting it go while there's a breath in my body.

Fay You mean while there's a breath in his body, don't you?

Howard backs nervously into the room idly wafting the croquet mallet

Raynor follows Howard on, holding Sam's holdall

Howard Ah, Mr Raynor, I was just contemplating a game of croquet; you wouldn't care to make up a four?

Raynor Not my game, John — I'm more for physical contact sports ... (*He stares grimly at Sam*)

Sam Perhaps you'd care for a drink? We're making some sangria.

Raynor I thought you were Spanish.

Sam Spanish? What made you think that?

Raynor You were talking Spanish.

Sam My wife and I like to practise our Spanish. We talk it all the time.

Raynor You're not talking it now — Mr Spencer.

Sam No, this is our English period; you've come just at the right time. (*He stops*) You know my name.

Raynor Yeh, I know your name. (*Pause*) Look, I'm sorry to disturb you yet again and I'm covered in embarrassment but I still haven't got my holdall. Although I'm now in possession of some exceptional leisure wear and a cashmere sweater of exquisite taste — I would prefer my own holdall. So I'm returning it to you, Mr Spencer.

Raynor thrusts the holdall into Sam's hands

Sam Er, how do you know it's mine?

Raynor It also contained your library book. Inside the book was a rate demand — a red notice — unpaid — used as a book mark. It gave me your name and address. Now, since I've returned your holdall perhaps you'd be kind enough to return mine …

Sam I only wish I could.

Raynor (*sharply*) What?

Sam But I haven't got it.

Raynor (*stepping forward*) Haven't got it?

Sam No.

Raynor Then what holdall did you take from the airport?

Sam Pardon?

Raynor (*nodding at Howard*) He took your holdall, I took his — so what holdall did you take?

Sam I didn't.

Raynor (*loudly*) Didn't!

Dodie enters with a jug of sangria and glasses on a tray

Howard Ah. Here's Dodie with the sangria. I really enjoy a glass after the heat of the day …

Howard pours a glass of sangria and hands it to Raynor

Raynor Looks like blood …

Howard Yes …

Raynor looks at the others suspiciously, noting that the other glasses are not being filled. Howard hastily pours a modest amount in the other glasses. Raynor drains his glass; the others hold their glasses anxiously and watch him. Howard hastily pours him another from the jug. Fay moves to drink her sangria but Sam quietly restrains her. Fay stares

Raynor There's something I don't understand, John. Why did you leave the airport without your holdall and without reporting it missing?
Sam (*desperately*) Why did I leave without my holdall?
Raynor Yes.
Sam Why did I leave the airport without my holdall and without reporting it missing?
Raynor That's what I said.
Howard (*quickly*) Because he thought I had it.
Raynor What?
Howard Dodie and I were late at Gatwick and we didn't all meet up until Alicante. And Sam didn't realize I had an identical holdall to his. When he saw me carrying it he thought it was his.
Raynor Why should you carry his holdall?
Howard What?
Raynor Why should he think you'd carry his holdall?
Howard (*desperately*) Why should he think I'd carry his holdall?
Raynor Yes.
Sam I thought Howard was mindful of my recent hernia operation. I thought "Good old Howard — he's carrying my holdall."
Raynor (*drinking*) I see. So what we're talking about here are two holdalls not three?
Howard Yes. Yours is probably circling Madrid at the moment — you know how things are.
Raynor (*to Sam*) But if you thought he had your holdall — why didn't you say something when he handed it to me?
Sam Why didn't I say something when he handed it to you …?

All except Raynor sip their drinks nervously then remember the sangria's drugged. Raynor suspiciously watches the following as he drains his second glass. Sam coughs and splutters and prevents Fay drinking. Again, Fay looks surprised

Howard looks around with pouched cheeks then exits

Dodie returns a mouthful of liquid daintily to her glass

Dodie Oh, a fly! (*She moves to the terrace door with her glass and hurls the liquid across the terrace*)

As Dodie throws the drink, Howard enters, his mouth drained

The drink strikes Howard

Raynor I'm waiting for an answer, John. Why didn't you say something?
Fay Because my husband already had his doubts. He said to me "I hope
   Howard hasn't got an identical holdall to mine because that would mean
   I've left my holdall at the airport."
Raynor But Howard was the one that left his holdall at the airport — and he
   was giving me your holdall in exchange for his! So why didn't you say
   something?
Sam Why didn't I say something?
Fay Because my husband has no confidence. He's lost both his parents this
   year and he's also suffered a sideways demotion. He just assumed the
   holdall must be yours.
Raynor Well, it wasn't.
Howard (*topping up Raynor's glass*) Never mind. I'm sure you'll get it
   back. As I said that money's probably circling Madrid at this very moment.

Silence

Raynor Money? Who said anything about money?
Howard Didn't someone mention money?
Raynor No.
Howard I'm sure I heard the word money …
Sam I thought I heard money mentioned. Did anyone mention money?
Dodie I said I thought it might be money.
Fay Yes, I heard Dodie say that.
Howard That's where I heard it. Is it money?
Raynor (*after a pause*) Only half a million in used notes …

*They all outdo each other in expressions of surprise. Howard even manages
an incredulous whistle*

Fay But wasn't that rather foolish sending it through baggage control — it
   could have been stolen.
Raynor It was stolen.
Howard We don't know that — it could be mislaid …
Raynor I meant it was stolen in the first place.
Howard Stolen!
Raynor Perhaps you've read about the violent robbery that took place on the
   North Circular yesterday — and its bloody aftermath.
Sam You don't mean the money came from that?

Raynor Yes. A robbery carried out by ruthless men dedicated to violence; and anyone who crosses them …

Sam Crosses them?

Raynor As good as dead …

Silence

Raynor rubs a weary hand across his brow

Howard You look tired, Mr Raynor; perhaps you'd like a dip in the pool …

Raynor I don't swim.

Howard I could teach you …

Raynor No, I haven't the time …

Howard (*picking up a croquet mallet and moving behind Raynor with it*) More time than you think … (*He raises the mallet behind Raynor, measuring up for the blow*)

Dodie, Sam and Fay stare at the upraised mallet

Dodie When you say you haven't the time, do you mean you're on the run?

Raynor No, I'm on duty. I'm a police officer.

Howard remains motionless in mid-strike

Fay Police officer!

Raynor Detective Inspector Raynor.

Howard gently puts the mallet down

Sam What are you doing here?

Raynor We had information that the money was coming to Spain through Alicante and that Chummy was passing himself off as a holiday-maker on a package tour. So acting on this information I took an earlier scheduled flight from Heathrow — to meet the incoming flight from Gatwick. And that's where our paths crossed …

Sam Why didn't you tell us you were a police officer?

Raynor Because, to tell the truth, I wasn't sure about you two. You could have been involved.

Howard (*with well-bred astonishment*) Inv … olved.

Raynor Accomplices. Why not? An out-of-work actor and a man with an unpaid rate demand — that's the raw material they work with.

Fay (*anxiously*) And what do you think now?

Raynor (*wearily*) Tell the truth, I don't know what to think — I'm too tired. It's been a long day. I remember seeing you all by the carousel and then I saw him …

Sam Chummy?

Raynor Yes. I was about to make an arrest but I reckoned without those package holiday-makers; they were like barbarians.

Howard I agree. I usually travel on a scheduled flight whenever possible.

Raynor I made a grab at him but I lost him in the crowd. I thought I'd got his holdall but it turned out to be full of duff videos.

Howard Duff!

Sam And you think we had something to do with all this?

Raynor Well, perhaps not. (*He regards them*) You're hardly the typical associates of Mad Dog Moon …

Silence

Sam Sorry? Mad Dog … ?

Raynor Moon.

Howard Mad Dog Moon!

Dodie The axe man?

Raynor The same.

Fay Not the one who bit the police dog at the Pizza Parlour siege?

Raynor That's him.

Sam You mean the one who impaled the security guard on the railings outside NatWest?

Raynor I'm afraid so — but don't think he lacks subtlety. He was the one who put the electrodes on Foaming Frankie Bennet.

Howard The Bermondsey torture trial!

Raynor Yes. He put those electrodes everywhere — and I mean everywhere. Frankie was never the same again. Mad Dog always had this fascination with electricity — and the private parts …

Fay And you saw him at Alicante?

Raynor Yes. I just hope he didn't see you.

Howard You think he might come here?

Raynor No — there'd be no point. Not if you haven't got the money. Pity; you were the only lead I had. He could be half-way to Madrid by now. (*Wearily*) I'd better phone in …

Fay But what if he comes? What does he look like?

Raynor Don't worry; you'll know Mad Dog Moon if you meet him. I only met him once and the experience was chilling; he emanates evil. And he has this twitch.

Howard Twitch?

Raynor As if he's got a stiff neck. (*He demonstrates*)

The others unconsciously do the same

He can't suppress it — no matter how he tries … Well, I'd better be going …

Raynor makes several attempts to put the glass back on the table, reaching further and further forward each time. The others watch him. He finally succeeds and then rolls on to the floor. No-one moves. Raynor gets to his feet in silence. He crosses the room in exaggerated slow motion, approaching first one exit and then another with staring eyes. The others watch in fascination

Fay takes Raynor's arm

Fay I think you've had too much sangria, Inspector.
Sam Would you like to rest for a while?
Raynor No … Phone in car … Rest there …
Fay You mustn't drive …
Sam We'll see you to the car …

Fay and Sam assist Raynor from the room

Howard and Dodie regard each other

Howard Well, Dodie — things are beginning to move our way.
Dodie Are they?
Howard I think the Inspector believes us.
Dodie He was drugged to the eyeballs, Howard.
Howard I agree he was confused but by the time those two had finished, so was I. They're mad, of course. They suffer from a collective insanity so common in long marriages — and the one advantage of working with idiots is that no-one would think they were clever enough to steal half a million.
Dodie So we are going to steal it?
Howard No, it's going to fall into our laps, Dodie.
Dodie Howard, we don't even know where the money is. The idiots do, but we don't.
Howard (*looking out into the garden*) It's in the garden somewhere …
Dodie They said they'd share it with us.
Howard That's not the point. The point is: are we going to share it with them? The trouble is two hundred and fifty thousand doesn't go very far these days.
Dodie How would you know?
Howard Because I've spent it, Dodie — more than once — on my rapacious

wives. That's why I'm broke and I'm tired of waiting for the part that never comes, waiting all morning for that phone to ring, not bothering to shave because it would leave me nothing to do in the afternoon. Well, I'm not waiting any longer. I want it now, Dodie.

Dodie But where is it?

Howard She'll tell me — just leave us alone.

Dodie Fay? You mean she's going to be exposed to your well-worn charms …

Howard Well-worn! All right — I know I look old … (*He pauses*) I said I know I look old.

Dodie You don't look old, Howard. But what about Fay. She looks past it to me.

Howard Past it. That's the mistake young people always make. They judge by appearances. Just because she doesn't keep her pies in the window — it doesn't mean she's stopped cooking …

Dodie What about Sam?

Howard His have been in the window too long ——

Dodie I mean won't he object?

Howard Just go into the garden — he'll follow. He'll want to keep an eye on the loot …

Sam and Fay enter

Sam He's asleep in the car.

Fay I wish he'd stayed here.

Howard Why?

Fay Why? Because of Mad Dog Moon.

Howard If he was coming he'd have been here by now, Fay.

Sam We don't even know if Raynor's a policeman. He could have made the whole thing up.

Howard Sam's right.

Sam The thing is not to lose our nerve.

Dodie walks on to the terrace

Where are you going, Dodie?

Dodie pauses

Dodie (*after a pause*) I thought I'd take a look around the garden …

Sam (*quickly*) I'll come with you — you shouldn't be alone …

Dodie exits; Sam follows her off

Fay sits on the settee. Howard joins her

Howard (*smiling*) Sam's certainly changed. Much more dynamic. Much
    more positive.
Fay It's the money.
Howard I rather like him, you know.
Fay (*surprised*) Do you?
Howard I only wished he liked me more ... (*Silence*) The thing I like most
    about you two is you're so genuine — whereas in my profession they're
    always acting.
Fay What about Dodie? Is she always acting?
Howard Between ourselves, Fay, she never stops. Life's one long audition.
Fay Isn't it for you?
Howard Is that why you distrust me? Because I'm an actor. You think I lack
    sincerity?
Fay Well, you have been married three times.
Howard And you think that makes me shallow?
Fay Well, did you love them?
Howard (*indignantly*) Well, it wasn't because I liked wedding cake!
Fay But three times. Sam said what do you do about maintenance?
Howard I've never asked for a penny, Fay. (*He touches her cheek*) Funny
    — I hadn't noticed that little freckle before ...
Fay Sam meant, what did you have to pay them? He's very interested in the
    financial side ...
Howard Pay them! They earned more than I did — and they'd taken all mine.
    They crushed me like a grape, Fay. There was nothing left for a second
    pressing. And when the money went, so did they. They weren't like you,
    Fay ... (*He glances towards the terrace*) You'd have stayed. No matter
    how *rough* and *unpleasant* things became — you'd have seen it through.

Fay follows Howard's glance

Fay You're talking about Sam — aren't you?
Howard I can sense the tension between you.
Fay He's certainly changed ...
Howard Tell me where the money is and he'll never see it again.
Fay He'd never forgive me.
Howard I wouldn't take it for myself. I'd leave it in Raynor's car while he
    was asleep. You're right — we're better off without that money, Fay. It's
    caused nothing but trouble.
Fay But you're broke.
Howard I've been broke before.
Fay Why are you doing this?

Howard Because of you, Fay. I've been drawn to you ever since we met, you must have noticed. Oh, I know there's no future for us, and no good will come of it. But I can't bear to see you unhappy. I love the way that little curl dangles there ... Where is the money, Fay? It hurts that you don't trust me ...

Fay How do I know you're not acting now? Pretending to like me.

Howard Pretending? You think this is pretence?

Fay I saw you with Vena Valance in *Sweet Bird of Youth*.

Howard (*pleased*) You saw me in that?

Fay Yes. You were all over her like a rash — and it all started by you teasing her hair ...

Howard stops teasing

Howard That was acting; I hardly knew her.

Fay Hardly knew her? You had your hand up her drawers.

Howard That was the director's idea.

Fay I thought it was yours. It said in the Sunday papers that you crept back to her dressing-room after the show and gave her one. Was that the director's idea, too?

Howard (*appalled*) Gave her one! That was idle gossip. Vena and I had no feelings for each other.

Fay You must have done ... All that kissing — and writhing — and thrusting — and grinding ...

Howard Fay, she as about as exciting as a plate of cold spaghetti.

Fay But you were kissing passionately.

Howard That was a stage kiss, Fay. No emotion whatsoever. Here. Let me show you.

Howard seizes Fay unexpectedly and kisses her long and hard. He releases her. She falls back, dazed

Do you see what I mean?

Fay (*dazed*) Yes. (*She clears her throat*) So that's a stage kiss. I've often wondered ... (*She rises, knocking over a sangria glass*)

Howard No emotion whatsoever ...

Fay I noticed that. Where's my handbag?

Howard Er, you're holding it, Fay.

Fay (*faintly*) So I am ... (*She opens her handbag*)

Howard Now, if you'd like me to show you the real thing ...

Fay No, that's all right. It was definitely different ...

Howard What are you looking for?

Fay Stiplick.

Sam appears on the terrace and stares suspiciously into the room

(*Seeing Sam*) Ah, Sam, there you are there … I mean, there you are, Sam … there.

Howard (*smiling*) I think I'll get a cigar. Smoke it on the terrace …

Howard exits into the hall

Fay continues to burrow into her handbag. Sam watches her

Sam You look as if you're going to crawl into that handbag … What happened?
Fay Nothing.
Sam Was he trying to find out where you'd put the money?
Fay Yes.
Sam And I suppose he was using all his charm to persuade you. Well, I just hope he doesn't try that sort of thing on me.
Fay (*sharply*) I don't think there's much danger of that, Sam.

Fay exits in the direction of the bedroom, slamming the door behind her. As she goes:

Dodie enters

Dodie Have you had an argument?
Sam Not really.
Dodie Is it because of Howard?
Sam What made you say that?
Dodie That's the sort of thing he'd do. Come between man and wife. He's done it before.
Sam Then why did you come away with him?
Dodie It seemed a good idea at the time.
Sam And now you regret it?
Dodie I think he only did it to spite Sidney. If Sidney found out about this I'd be looking for another agent.
Sam And you don't think it's worth that?
Dodie Not really …

Dodie stalks Sam round the room during the following; he tries to keep his distance

Not when I realized that what excited Howard was not the effect I was having on him but the effect he was having on me …

Sam (*embarrassed*) Oh.

Dodie finally traps Sam by the cabinet; by the end of the following speech she is almost pressed against him

Dodie He never stops watching himself. He's like a poltergeist, he feeds off the energy of others. Someone once told him that his acting style was laid back; since then he's been practically horizontal. He just lies there. You wouldn't just lie there — would you, Sam … ?

Sam has little choice but to kiss her

   (*With feigned surprise*) Why did you do that?
Sam I don't know.
Dodie You must have had a reason.
Sam I lost both my parents this year.
Dodie And it made you realize how short life is?
Sam Well, they were in their nineties.
Dodie But you suddenly realized this is it, this is all we've got — it isn't a rehearsal.
Sam (*hoarsely*) Yes.
Dodie That's how I feel.

Dodie kisses Sam

   You do like me a little, don't you?
Sam Yes.
Dodie What hurts me is that you don't trust me.
Sam I trust you, Dodie — it's him.
Dodie Yes. It would serve Howard right if you and I split the money and as the Spanish say — vamoosed.

A faint slyness creeps into Sam's eyes

Sam Dodie, if I were to tell you where the money is …
Dodie Yes?
Sam You could get it while I kept the others talking.
Dodie That's a good idea. Well — where is it, Sam?
Sam It's at the foot of the steps on the left-hand side — deep in the bougainvillaea.
Dodie The left?
Sam Yes.

Dodie looks at her hands

Why are you looking at your hands?

Dodie I have trouble with right and left. Left's the hand with the rings on. Now — is it left facing me or me facing left?

Sam For God's sake, Dodie. (*He points*) It's down there!

Howard enters smoking a cigar

(*Dropping his arm*) Ah, Howard. Can I get you a drink? (*He moves to the cabinet*)

Howard Thank you, Sam. Do you think I could have some ice?

Sam (*hesitating*) Ice. Yes ...

Sam exits to the kitchen

Howard He's told you, hasn't he?

Dodie Didn't she tell you?

Howard She would have done. She didn't have time. Well, where is it?

Dodie (*smiling*) I don't have to tell you. I could keep the money for myself.

Howard You wouldn't.

Dodie Wouldn't I?

Howard Dodie, don't you realize with all this money I could leave Rachel and come to you? Have you thought about that? I could afford another divorce, Dodie.

Dodie Yes. Strange but I don't find that argument quite as persuasive as you do. I wonder why?

Howard Then I'll give you another argument. You'll need me to drive the car; you can't drive on the continent, they drive on the hand-without-the-rings side. And then there's Mad Dog Moon — you'll need me to protect you. It's still a man's world, Miss Cheese Spread.

Dodie (*after a hesitation*) It's down there, at the foot of the steps — in the bougainvillaea ...

Howard descends the terrace steps and exits into the garden

Sam returns with ice

Dodie moves to Sam

Sam Where's Howard?

Dodie Smoking his cigar in the garden. He didn't want to pollute the atmosphere – I thought it was a little late for that, but there you are. No, don't call him; I love these moments alone with you, Sam ... (*She puts a hand on his arm*)

Fay enters and regards Sam and Dodie suspiciously

Ah, here's Fay …

There is a loud cry, off, followed by an equally loud splash. Sam, Dodie and Fay stare at each other and then make a dash for the end of the terrace. They look down at the pool. There are the sounds of heavy splashing

Sam It's Howard. He must have dived in the pool.
Fay But he's still got his clothes on.
Dodie Well, I know he didn't want to get sunburnt but that's going too far.
Sam He's swimming very fast, considering …
Fay And he's still smoking his cigar.
Dodie It must have been a last-minute decision …
Sam Unless something frightened him …

Sam and Fay look at each other. There is a squelching sound. Sam, Fay and Dodie stand back from the steps

Howard appears up the steps. He is dripping wet with his cigar still clenched between his teeth

Howard removes the cigar

Howard Snakes.

Howard exits with as much dignity as he can muster

Curtain

Scene 2

The villa. Late evening

When the Curtain *rises, the lights have been switched on on the terrace. The television set is on, with a low hum of sound*

Dodie sits watching the TV

Howard enters wearing a dressing-gown and carrying a towel

Dodie (*looking up*) How do you feel now?
Howard Better. I've rested and showered — and now I feel ready for anything. Where are they?

Dodie Down by the pool.

Howard I thought so. Keeping an eye on the money.

Dodie (*drily*) I thought the snake was doing that?

Howard Don't mention the snake. I don't want to think about it. All the time I was in the shower I thought it was going to come up the plughole.

Dodie (*worried*) It wouldn't come into the house, would it?

Howard Wouldn't it? Remember "The Speckled Band"? It came down the bloody bellrope. You could find a snake in bed with you tomorrow morning.

Dodie So what's new?

Howard I think your humour's getting a little rancid, darling. What are you watching?

Dodie One of your old videos.

Howard (*surprised and delighted*) Oh. Is it a good part?

Dodie Not really. You don't say much but then you wouldn't.

Howard Why not?

Dodie You're dead.

Howard Dead! (*He looks closer*)

Dodie See. You're on a slab, in the morgue — dead.

Howard So I am. But don't I look young? No — don't switch it off.

Dodie But you're not saying anything.

Howard Be fair, Dodie — how can I say anything? I'm dead. It gets better.

Dodie You mean you go to heaven?

Howard No, there's a flashback — explaining how I came to be shot. Why were you watching?

Dodie I was curious. I wanted to see what I missed. When you were young and vibrant.

Howard And what do you think?

Dodie I can't see any difference. You're just lying there.

Howard You wait for the flashback.

Dodie I don't like flashbacks.

Howard (*sadly*) Neither do I. Most people only see photographs of themselves when they were young. I see the whole thing — talking, laughing, leaping, dancing. I was in a bar in Florence last year. They had a television on. And suddenly I thought "I know that man." It was me, not only looking good and full of youth and vitality but also speaking perfect Italian, a thing I've never been able to do before. And I looked around the bar and realized that no-one knew me. I felt like the picture of Dorian Gray. That's why I need the money, Dodie.

Dodie Don't start that again, Howard.

Howard You can get it. Just wait for them to come in.

Dodie Howard, I'm terrified of snakes.

Howard You don't have to be.

Dodie Why not?

Howard They don't bite women.

Dodie (*staring*) How do you know?

Howard It's a fact.

Dodie You've just made it up.

Howard No. It didn't bite Fay, did it?

Dodie That doesn't mean snakes don't bite women. I think I'd need a little more evidence than that. In the history of snake biting I'm sure women have figured as large as men. (*Pause*) What about Cleopatra?

Howard She asked for it. (*He sighs*) All right. But surely if Fay had the courage to put the holdall there surely you have the courage to retrieve it. What sort of woman are you?

Dodie What sort of man are you?

Howard You don't understand. I got on the wrong side of it. I startled it.

Dodie I thought it startled you. (*She hesitates*) What was it like?

Howard Just an ordinary snake really. It was coiled around the holdall. It looked at me and sort of yawned — and I panicked.

Dodie I'm surprised. You've never been frightened of yawning before, Howard. Remember how they yawned at Frinton when you did *An Inspector Calls*?

Howard (*frowning*) And then it hissed.

Dodie They did that too.

Howard I mean it took a personal dislike to me.

Dodie So did Frinton.

Howard Will you stop talking about Frinton! Ah. Here's the flashback.

They watch the set closely

Well, what do you think?

Dodie I think I preferred you on the slab. Are you sure that's you?

Howard Of course it's me. I haven't changed that much.

Dodie No but you've got a stocking over your head.

Howard That's because I'm robbing a bank.

Dodie I wouldn't have known you.

Howard (*thoughtfully*) Wouldn't you? (*He switches off the set*)

Dodie I thought you wanted to watch?

Howard Dodie, suppose I told you that we could have that money — in fact, they'd give it to us — and no-one would know we'd got it … ?

Dodie Of course they'd know we'd got it — and they'd certainly never give it to us.

Howard No but they'd give it to Mad Dog Moon … (*He imitates Mad Dog Moon's twitch of the neck*) They'd be petrified …

Dodie They'd know you.

Howard Not with a stocking over my face they wouldn't. They'd think Mad
  Dog had come for his money. And that's what they'd tell the police. No-
  one would ever know.
Dodie Mad Dog Moon would know. What happens when they catch him?
Howard He's going to say he hasn't got the money but he'd say that anyway.
  Who's going to believe him, Dodie?
Dodie You're right. It's perfect. If you can do it.
Howard Of course I can do it. Just get me a pair of your tights ...

Howard leads Dodie to the door

Dodie Where are you going to be while all this is happening?
Howard Resting. Worn out by the events of the day.

Dodie hesitates

  What's the matter?
Dodie You won't ham it up, will you, Howard?
Howard (*shocked*) Ham it up? I've never hammed anything up in my life.
Dodie Howard, (*she nods towards the television*) you were even hamming
  it up on that slab ...

Howard and Dodie exit

Sam puts his head around the door

Sam They've gone.

Sam enters, followed by Fay

Fay Where?
Sam (*darkly*) Probably the bedroom ...
Fay Don't sound so aggrieved.
Sam I'm not. It suits our purpose. Now, get the money and let's get out of
  here.
Fay No, Sam.
Sam Why not?
Fay Because I don't want to go back to England in handcuffs. How would
  it look, Sam? What will people say? We're members of Neighbourhood
  Watch.
Sam All that's behind us, Fay. I've changed.
Fay I know and before I came here I thought any change would be an
  improvement; now I'm not so sure.
Sam I've told you, Fay — I'm going all the way.

Fay If you're going all the way you get the money.

Sam I've told you — I can't stand snakes.

Fay Then you haven't changed that much, have you?

Sam Neither have you. You may not be frightened of snakes but you're certainly frightened of that money.

Fay You're right. I always thought you stayed with me because you didn't fancy other women but I've been watching you ... It's not other women you didn't fancy — it was taking out a second mortgage.

Dodie enters. She crosses theatrically to the terrace and gives a display of suppressed agitation

Sam and Fay watch Dodie curiously

Sam Where's Howard?

Dodie Sleeping ... (*She peers out into darkness and becomes even more agitated*)

Fay What's the matter, Dodie?

Dodie I was drawing the curtains and I thought I saw someone ... Someone down there by the gazebo — a shadowy figure — skulking.

Sam Skulking?

Dodie I thought — could it be Mad Dog Moon?

Fay gasps

Sam No, I'm sure you're mistaken, Dodie.

Dodie I do hope so, Sam. I just can't bear the thought of those electrodes. Tell me he's not out there ... (*She turns away in fear*)

Sam (*moving on to the terrace and looks over it*) No, I can't see anyone ...

Moon, a small, dapper man, appears on the terrace behind Sam. He is carrying a light raincoat over his arm

I think it was your imagination.

Dodie Pray God it was ——

Sam turns and sees the newcomer

Sam Oh, there is someone ...

Dodie I knew it! (*She turns and looks surprised*) Oh!

Moon Good-evening, sir. I'm sorry to disturb you at this time of night ...

Sam Who are you?

Moon (*showing his identity card*) Detective Inspector Raynor. New Scotland Yard.

Sam But he's out in the car.

Moon (*smiling*) You didn't really believe that, did you, sir?

Sam Didn't I?

Moon Of course you didn't or you'd have given him the money, wouldn't you? I really must congratulate you on your perception. Although I must say he was hardly convincing — in fact it was a lamentable attempt to impersonate a police officer.

Fay But if he's not a police officer, who is he?

Moon You'd perhaps know him better as — Mad Dog Moon.

Dodie Mad Dog Moon! (*She peers out anxiously across the terrace*)

Moon (*watching her curiously*) Don't be alarmed. We've taken him into custody. You won't see him again tonight.

Dodie Are you sure?

Moon Yes, we've got him. He didn't put up much of a struggle — in fact, he seemed quite worn out. Still, you've had a lucky escape and we are in your debt. I don't know where we'd be without the vigilance of the general public … (*He smiles at the others pleasantly*)

Sam (*shrugging*) It was nothing …

Moon It was everything, sir. Now, if you'd just let me have the money ——

Fay makes to speak

Sam (*quickly*) We'd love to but we haven't got it.

Moon (*his smile fading*) Haven't got it?

Sam No. There was some confusion over our holdalls at the airport and he thought we'd got the money — but we haven't …

Moon No money?

Sam No, but everyone seems to think we have. It's hilarious, isn't it?

Moon Hilarious? Then why aren't I laughing?

Sam Because you're disappointed.

Moon You could say that. You see, I saw you take the holdall ——

Sam No, you thought you saw me take the holdall; that's where the confusion came in.

Moon I wasn't confused; there was a red thread around the handle of the holdall and you took it. I saw you.

Sam I see. So there was a red thread round your holdall as well, was there?

Moon What?

Sam Sangria, Inspector … ? (*He turns towards the drinks cabinet*)

Moon suddenly twists his neck in an exaggerated twitch, as if heading an imaginary football. Fay and Dodie see the twitch but Sam remains blissfully unaware

Moon No, I'm on duty.

Dodie edges nervously towards the terrace

   (*Sharply*) No. Don't go, miss.
Fay I'll have one, darling ... (*She moves to the drinks cabinet*)
Sam (*surprised*) You'll have one?
Fay Yes. (*She mouths silently*) He's Mad Dog Moon.
Sam (*mouthing silently back*) He's what?
Fay (*silently*) He's Mad Dog Moon.
Sam (*silently*) Mad Dog Moon? (*He stares uncomprehendingly*)
Moon (*moving between Fay and Sam*) I think she's trying to tell you I'm Mad
   Dog Moon ...
Sam (*still mouthing silently*) Mad Dog Moon?

Moon twitches again

   My God! You're Mad Dog Moon.
Moon (*sharply*) How did you guess? What is it about me? Do I look mad?
Sam (*hastily*) No.
Moon Then why do they call me mad?
Sam I don't know.
Moon How many "O" levels did you get?
Sam Three.
Moon I got six. (*Sharply*) What's the capital of Poland?
Sam (*staring wildly*) I don't remember.
Moon Warsaw. Seven eights?
Sam I can't think.
Moon Fifty-six. And you call me mad. I'm half-way through an Open
   University course in English Lit. Does that seem mad to you?
Sam No.
Moon (*twitching*) Then what gave me away?
Sam Nothing. It was just a wild guess. In fact I find you refreshingly normal.
Moon (*after a pause*) Of course, there are advantages in being called mad
   ... People listen ——
Sam We're certainly listening.
Moon — and they do what I tell them ——
Sam I can believe that.
Moon — and their memories improve ...
Sam Now that surprises me. I couldn't remember the capital of Poland.
Moon Ah, but you see, your life wasn't depending on it, was it?
Sam (*gulping*) Life?
Moon I want that ——

Suddenly Howard bounds in from the terrace with a muffled shout; the muffling is due to a pair of tights pulled over his face and a small handkerchief he has put in his mouth to disguise his voice. He has changed into black polo-neck shirt, jeans and sneakers. He is carrying a small kitchen meat mallet which he brandishes. He makes several muffled speeches that no-one can understand. He points this way and that but is totally incomprehensible

Sam We can't understand you.

Howard hesitates, then rolls up his stocking slightly and removes the handkerchief from his mouth

Howard (*menacingly*) Everybody settle down and be quiet …
Moon We are quiet.
Howard You'd better be because if you're not, John, I'll get frustrated — know what I mean? Then I'll get one of my blinding headaches … (*He twitches*) Then I can turn very, very nasty … (*He stops, realizing there's a stranger in the room. He moves towards Moon and stumbles against the furniture. He peers through the stocking*) Who are you?
Moon (*calmly*) I'm the pool man.
Howard Pool man. (*He taps the mallet in his hand*) Isn't it rather late for the pool man?
Moon I was concerned about the growth of body algae. It couldn't wait until morning.
Howard I see. Well, just be quiet.
Moon I am quiet.
Howard And keep still.
Moon I am still.
Howard Don't cross me, John. (*He turns to Sam*) Now, John.
Moon Yes?
Howard Not you. Him. (*He motions to Sam*)
Moon I thought I was John?
Howard Not now! Just keep out of this, pool man. (*To Sam*) Now, John, I'm going to ask you to bring the money to me now. If you don't we're talking GBH; we're talking serious injury, John. You know who I am, don't you?
Moon No — who are you?
Howard (*turning sharply*) I won't warn you again! You know who I am, John?
Sam I think so …
Howard So — if you don't get me the money ...

Howard takes Fay's arm

... it's going to be very bad news for your wife — and her future physical well-being ... (*He brandishes the meat mallet*) Know what this is, John?

Sam (*politely*) It looks like a sort of meat mallet ...

Howard It is a meat mallet — for pounding meat ... Get my drift, John?

Moon It doesn't look much of a weapon.

Howard (*moving to Moon*) What did you say?

Moon I said, it doesn't look much of a weapon — a meat mallet.

Howard It has a serrated metal edge ...

Moon It's a kitchen implement.

Howard I'm improvising. Now, listen, John ——

Moon John? Are you talking to me now — or are you talking to him?

Howard I'm talking to you. Don't try my patience too far. (*He gives a massive twitch*)

Moon responds with a twitch

Are you mocking me?

Moon No.

Howard I wouldn't, John. An attitude like that could prove fatal. I'm getting very angry ... I'm getting the red mist, John.

Moon Are you? Well, you won't do much damage with that — an ordinary kitchen meat mallet ...

Howard Suddenly everyone's an expert. And what would you use, John?

Moon I'd use this ... (*He takes a small hatchet from the inside pocket of his mac*)

There's an intake of breath   Loose Fay

Howard (*staring*) You're Mad Dog Moon.

Moon That's right.

Moon pulls the stocking from Howard's face

And who are you?

Howard I'm Howard Booth. The actor.

Moon (*surprised*) You're an actor?

Howard Yes.

Moon I don't believe it.

Dodie (*quietly*) They didn't at Frinton.

Howard Don't you recognize me?

Moon (*studying Howard's face*) No. In fact, I preferred you with the stocking on ... (*He shakes his head*) That was a terrible performance.

Howard Well, I was just getting into it.

Moon It lacked conviction, it had no subtlety, and it was wildly over the top. Who were you supposed to be?

Howard (*hastily*) No-one.

Moon Then what were you doing? Do you normally leap into a room with a stocking over your head and brandishing a meat mallet just when the mood takes you?

Howard Well, no ——

Moon You're not a kissogram, are you?

Howard Certainly not. We were playing a game.

Moon A game? What game? Perhaps I can join in ...

Howard It was "In the manner of the word".

Moon And what was the word?

Howard Menacingly.

Moon Menacingly! You had about as much menace as a two-day-old meringue. I've known cocker spaniels with more menace. Do you mind if I give you some advice?

Howard Not at all.

Moon Never raise your voice and cut down on the gestures; move more slowly; invest it with a little humour as a sort of counterpoint to the horrors to come. Make them laugh, make them cry — but above all, make them wait. So that when it finally comes, it's almost a relief ...

Sam (*nervously*) When what finally comes?

Moon You'll soon find out — if I don't get my money.

Fay Your money? You stole it.

Moon What makes you think that?

Fay Why else would you bring all this money into Spain?

Moon I'm investing in property.

Fay With half a million in cash?

Moon I'm a first-time buyer.

Sam We thought it may have come from the robbery ...

Moon (*sharply*) Robbery?

Howard The armoured car robbery.

Sam (*soothingly*) We're not blaming you, Mad Dog. We're on your side. We didn't tell the police, did we? We know what you went through to get that money. We admire you.

Howard We think you earned it.

Moon (*slowly*) That's all right then ...

Sam But we think we deserve something for our efforts — and for keeping quiet.

Howard We're talking about a deal ... (*an affectionate diminutive*) Mad ——

Moon What sort of a deal?

Sam We thought you'd have the lion's share and we'd get fifty thousand each ...

Howard That's not too much to ask, is it, (*a more affectionate diminutive*) Maddie ... ?

Moon Isn't it?

Howard All right. Forget the women. Fifty thousand each for the men. Is that a deal?

Moon No. The deal is: I get the money and you don't walk away on stumps ...

Sam and Howard take a pace back

Fay (*sardonically*) Don't let him frighten you, Sam. Remember — you're going all the way.

Sam Shut up, Fay

Fay It's half a million pounds, Sam. You've waited all your life for a chance like this.

Moon moves close to Sam

Moon (*menacingly*) You think it's a lot of money?

Sam Well, yes.

Moon (*shaking his head*) It isn't — not to you. You've got it out of proportion — and I'm going to do you a favour: I'm going to show how little it's worth. It's not even worth a little pain, Sam. It's not even worth your little finger ...

Sam Little finger ... ?

Moon Where's that money?

Fast

Fay Don't tell him, Sam. He's bluffing.

Moon I'm not bluffing.

Sam He's not bluffing, Fay.

Fay He hasn't got the nerve.

Moon I've got the nerve.

Sam Fay, he's got the nerve — just keep out of this.

Moon (*moving to Fay*) No. If she wants to join it ...

Moon takes Fay's wrist

Think, Sam. You're settling down at home one evening. Your wife crosses to the piano. "What would you like me to play, dearest?" she asks. And you say, "Play the sonata, darling — you play it so well." She turns. There are tears in her eyes. "I can't play the sonata, darling," she rejoins, "not any more! You're forgetting — I can't span an octave ... "

Moon holds up Fay's hand

It would be heartbreaking, wouldn't it?

Fay (*coldly*) Not really — I don't play the piano.

Moon I was talking hypothetically.

Sam (*desperately*) Did you hear that, Fay? Hypothetically!

Moon raises the hatchet

Moon Well?

Sam (*quickly*) It's in the bougainvillaea — down by the pool.

Moon Get it.

Sam No.

Moon (*raising the hatchet*) Get it.

Sam All right. All right. I'll get it. Just give me a moment. (*He tucks his trousers into his socks and slip on the snorkel mask*)

Moon (*staring incredulously*)What's he doing?

Fay (*smiling*)There's no need for that, Sam. I've moved it. It's in the cabinet. (*She moves to the cabinet, takes out the holdall and gives it to Moon*)

Moon (*after a pause*) That's better.

Howard All right. What about twenty-five grand for each of the men? And we'll give you a head start.

Moon No, I'm giving you a head start — I'm leaving it on your shoulders …

Howard Oh.

Moon Now, before I check the money — and I know how much there should be — I'm going to declare an amnesty. That means anyone who's taken cash can return it, no questions asked. Otherwise you may find the body search objectionable … (*He opens the holdall*) I'm waiting …

Howard and Sam look at each other and sigh. They drop their bundles of money into the holdall. Dodie comes forward abruptly and drops her bundle in. The men look surprised

I have counted every note …

Howard sighs, turns his back on the holdall and removes a second bundle of money from his pocket. He drops it in the holdall

Any more … ?

Sam No, I'm sure that's it.

Fay comes forward. She opens her handbag and drops a large wad of money from it into the holdall

(*Looking shocked*) Fay!

Moon Now — let's see what we've got ... (*He puts down the hatchet and puts both hands into the holdall*)

There is a loud hiss, followed by a scream from Moon. His face twists in horror. He pulls his hands out of the holdall. He has a large snake attached to them

My God! Get him off me. (*He jumps up trying to throw the snake from him but it remains attached*)

The others all leap back and duck

Sam Not in here! Stop swinging around
Howard Outside! Throw it outside!
Moon It's hanging on!
Fay Hit it with something!
Howard (*picking up the meat mallet*) Keep still — I'll smash its head in!
Sam No — jump in the pool.
Dodie Drown it.
Moon I can't swim ...

The two couples hustle Moon out on to the terrace

Moon I can't get it off.
Sam Drown it in the pool. He goes to Kvrau (~~steps~~?)

They assit Moon down the steps during the following oldes follow him

Howard Keep still — I'll smash its head in ...
Moon My God! It's bitten me ...

Moon disappears down the steps. As he does so:

Howard raises the mallet

Howard Keep still! (*He brings the mallet downward*)

There are the sounds of a blow and of a body falling. Sam, Howard, Dodie and Fay look anxiously down the steps

Oh.

Sam (*quietly*) You were supposed to kill the snake, Howard — now he's got away.

Dodie Well, Moon hasn't — he's not going anywhere.
Fay He's very still.
Howard You don't think he's ... ?
Sam We'd better check ...

They all disappear down the steps

Raynor enters with two Spanish policemen

Raynor looks over the railings, then motions to the policemen

The policemen disappear down the steps

Raynor returns to the room, sees the holdall, moves to it and looks in

Sam, Howard, Fay and Dodie enter sheepishly from the terrace

Sam Ah. You've found the money, Inspector. Thank God.
Howard You don't know how difficult it's been keeping it from him.
Raynor Keeping it from him? I thought you were keeping it from me?

They all laugh at the absurdity of this notion

How is he? I should have gone down but I can't stand dead bodies.
Fay He's not dead but he's got a lot wrong with him.
Sam He's been bitten by a snake, he's been hit with a meat mallet and he's fallen down the steps, but he's still breathing. They're sending for an ambulance.
Raynor Then I'd better be going. I'll take your statements later. You could come out of this rather well.
Howard Will we get a reward?
Raynor Not that well.
Sam But we caught him.
Raynor You didn't give me the money.
Dodie We weren't sure who you were.
Fay You didn't seem like a policeman.
Howard (*muttering*) And you were drunk on the job ...

Raynor turns and moves to Howard

Raynor What was that?
Howard Inspector, I'm not being critical. We're both men of the world. If

he doesn't make it — and you never know with snake bites, or even meat mallets — who's to know about the money … ? I mean, why don't you take half — and we could split the other half between us. Who'd know?

Raynor I would … Mr Booth …

Raynor exits

Sam Howard — that was stupid.
Howard You're right. What a fool. (*Pause*) I should have offered him two thirds and something for the Federali. What do you think?

~~*Sam, Fay and Dodie rain cushions down on Howard*~~
Dodie

It was only a suggestion.
Dodie Well, I'm sick of your suggestions!

Dodie pushes Howard out of the way and exits to the hall

Howard Dodie!

Howard follows Dodie off

Sam (*wearily*) What a day.
Fay It could have been worse.
Sam How could it have been worse? I was worth half a million a few hours ago — now look at me.
Fay You weren't, Sam. And when it came down to it you didn't even think it was worth my little finger … (*She kisses Sam*)
Sam I suddenly remembered you were a typist.
Fay No ... you learned something today, didn't you?
Sam Yes, Warsaw's the capital of Poland.
Fay No, you learned that marriage still means something.
Sam Does it?
Fay Sam, my father's been dead seven years but whenever my mother mentions his name tears still come to her eyes.
Sam They did when he was alive, Fay.
Fay (*with a wry smile*) Oh, Sam.

They kiss

Howard enters

Howard What a girl! She never stops acting. She's pacing about outside like

Bette-bloody-Davis. She says all I can think about is the money. Me! In a life littered with tragic mistakes and monumental blunders she beats them all. And I was going to break my wife's heart for that woman. How could I have preferred her to Rachel?

Dodie enters

If you've come to apologize ...

Dodie It's Sidney!

Howard What?

Dodie He's in the drive. He can't get near the villa for police cars.

Howard Sidney! What's he doing here?

Dodie He's with a woman.

Fay It's not his wife — she's in Australia.

Sam And you said things couldn't get any worse.

Howard You know what's happened? He found out I'd cancelled and arranged a dirty weekend. The rat.

Dodie But what's he going to say?

Howard Nothing. What can he say? He can't afford to offend us. He's with another woman. Your job's safe, Fay. And he wouldn't dare tell Rachel or I might do some talking. And how can he be jealous of us, Dodie? He's having an affair!

Fay Howard's right. What can he do?

Sam Right. (*He relaxes*) Sangria, everyone?

Sam pours each of them a glass of sangria

Howard moves to the hall door

Dodie Is he coming?

Howard (*from the door*) Yes. He's probably carrying her over the threshold ...

They all laugh

Sam Here's to you, Sidney ...

They raise their glasses

Howard (*looking through the open door*) Hallo, Sidney ... (*Bantering*) Who's the lady friend? Do I know her? (*His smile fades*) My God! Rachel!

CURTAIN

FURNITURE AND PROPERTY LIST

ACT I

On stage: LIVING-ROOM
Bamboo and wicker furniture (armchairs, settee etc.) with cushions
Table. *On it*: **Fay**'s handbag containing phrase book
Drinks cabinet
Television set
Bags
Cases
Airport carrier bag containing mainly bottles
Blue holdall containing money

TERRACE
Table
Chairs
Beach bag. *In it*: snorkels, flippers, bathing hat
Balls
Croquet mallets
Sombrero on stand
Garden brush

Off stage: Cheese (**Sam**)
Blue holdall, rolled-up British newspaper (**Howard**)
Two cases, assorted bags (**Dodie**)
Drinks on a tray (**Howard**)
Blue holdall (**Raynor**)

Personal: **Sam**: key
Howard: key, dark glasses
Fay: handkerchief

ACT II
SCENE 1

Off stage: Jug of sangria and glasses on tray (**Dodie**)
Cigar (**Howard**)
Ice in ice bucket (**Sam**)
Sam's holdall (**Raynor**)

Personal: **Fay**: handbag

Scene 2

Set: In cabinet: holdall containing money and snake

Off stage: Towel (**Howard**)
               Light raincoat (**Moon**)
               Kitchen meat mallet (**Howard**)

Personal: **Moon**: identity card, small hatchet
               Howard: tights, handkerchief, two bundles of money
               Sam: bundle of money
               Dodie: bundle of money
               Fay: handbag containing bundle of money

LIGHTING PLOT

Practical fittings required: ornamental lights on terrace
A living-room and terrace with exterior backing. The same throughout

ACT I

To open: Bright general interior and exterior light; late summer afternoon effect

No cues

ACT II, SCENE 1

To open: As ACT I

No cues

ACT II, SCENE 2

To open: Late evening effect on terrace and exterior backing; lights on in living-room and practicals on terrace; TV flicker effect on

Cue 1   **Howard** switches off the TV set   (Page 54)
           Cut TV flicker effect

EFFECTS PLOT

ACT I

Cue 1   **Howard**: "Of course I'm right."   (Page 25)
Doorbell

ACT II

Cue 2   Loud cry, off   (Page 52)
Loud splash

Cue 3   **Sam**, **Dodie** and **Fay** look down at the pool   (Page 52)
Heavy splashing

Cue 4   When ACT II Scene 2 begins   (Page 52)
Low hum of TV sound

Cue 5   **Howard** switches off the TV set   (Page 54)
TV sound off

Cue 6   **Moon** puts his hands in the holdall   (Page 64)
Loud hiss

Cue 7   **Howard** brings the mallet downward   (Page 64)
Sounds of a blow and a body falling